ADIRONDACK BRIDGEBUILDER FROM CHARLESTON

ADIRONDACK BRIDGEBUILDER FROM CHARLESTON

THE LIFE AND TIMES OF
ROBERT CODGELL GILCHRIST

Rosemary Miner Pelkey

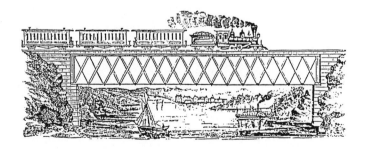

North Country Books
Utica, New York

The Life and Times of Robert Cogdell Gilchrist:
Adirondack Bridgebuilder from Charleston

ISBN 0-925168-23-8

Cover: Robert Cogdell Gilchrist at age twenty,
painted by George Cooke.
Courtesy of the Gibbes Museum of Art.

Library of Congress Cataloging-in-Publication Data

Pelkey, Rosemary Miner
    The life and times of Robert Cogdell Gilchrist :
Adirondack bridgebuilder from Charleston / by
Rosemary Miner Pelkey.
        p.   cm.
    Includes bibliographical references and index.
            ISBN 0-925168-23-8
    1. Gilchrist, Robert C. (Robert Cogdell), b.
1829.   2. Adirondack Park (N.Y.)—Biography.
3. Bridges—New York (State)—Adirondack Park
—History—19th century.   4. Charleston (S.C.)—
Biography.   I. Title.
F127.A2P44   1993
974.7'503'092—dc20
[B]   93-6165
                                                    CIP

Published by
NORTH COUNTRY BOOKS, INC.
PUBLISHER—DISTRIBUTOR
18 Irving Place
Utica, New York 13501

For Wes

Rosemary Miner Pelkey

A graduate of the State University of New York at Plattsburgh, and Union College, Rosemary Miner Pelkey turned to free-lance writing after nineteen years of teaching American Studies at Niskayuna High School. Her articles have appeared in *The Christian Science Monitor*, South Carolina Historical Society's *Carologue*, *Adirondack Life*, and other regional publications.

She is secretary of the Johnsburg Historical Society, a board member of the Lake George Arts Project, and president of the North Creek Railway Depot Preservation Association. She and her husband live in the Adirondack hamlet of Wevertown, New York.

Contents

Acknowledgments

It is a pleasure to acknowledge those who helped in the research and effort that went into this book. It could not have been written without Wevertown historian, Lewis Waddell, who is generous in sharing his time and his knowledge of the history of the area. He answered questions, shared books and materials, and suggested where to look for answers.

Mr. Richard S. Allen, author of several books, and most particularly *Old North Country Bridges*, was invaluable in that he shared so much of his knowledge of bridges, and suggested leads I could not have found on my own. After my first query, we exchanged letters and information and eventually met and looked at the bridge abutments and cables together. I owe him beyond words.

I am grateful to the many librarians and archivists who were helpful. Particularly the Crandall Library in Glens Falls, New York, their reference staff and Bruce Cole; the Adirondack Museum Librarian, Jerold Pepper; Chestertown historians, Jane Parrott and Pam Greco; Warren County historian, Pam Vogel; former Ironworks Consultant for Hudson-Mohawk Industrial Gateway, Edward Keyes; Staff of the Rensselaer Polytechnic Institute's Folsom Library Archives; the New York Historical Society; New York's Onondaga Historical Association; and New York State University Library at Albany.

I found Southern warmth and much professional help at the South Carolina Historical Society from their staff: Librarian Cam Alexander, Harlan Green, Mary Giles, Kathleen Howard and Steven Hoffius. Also Angela Mack of Charleston's Gibbes Museum; H.J. Harsook of the University of South Carolina archives; City of Charleston's Archives; the Robert Scott Small Library archives at the College of Charleston; Charleston's Library Society; the reference department of the Charleston County Library; and the Manuscript Department of the William Perkins Library at Duke University.

Individuals who answered queries and suggested leads or gave other help were Vicki Arnold; Augusta MacDowell Ball; James W. Brown, Jr.; Beverly Donald; Marie Fisher; Fred Gilchrist; Sterling Goodspeed; William Halsey; Bob E. James; Patricia Jordan; Celeste Kavanaugh; Jane Le-Count; David Newkirk; Warren Ripley; Robert N. Rosen; Anna Wells Rutledge; James Shaughnessy; Lou Sassi; Phil Sullivan; Roger Kennedy of the Smithsonian; and most particularly Professor Rayburn S. Moore of the University of Georgia, whose knowledge of the correspondence between Hayne and Gilchrist was so important.

Special thanks to the Monday writers of the Lake George Arts Project who listened and criticized some of the pages. The writer, Anne White, joined me on one Charleston trip and greatly assisted my research. My husband, Wes, walked miles with me in Charleston and the Adirondacks, took photographs, made lunches while I wrote, and gave me the kind of help that made all the difference. This is his book, too.

The Family

Robert Cogdell Gilchrist (1829-1902)
Charleston attorney, artist, author, Confederate officer and Adirondack bridgebuilder.

Adam Gilchrist (1760-1816)
Charleston shipping merchant and paternal grandfather of Robert Cogdell Gilchrist.

Robert August Gilchrist (1763-1817)
Adam's younger brother and New York shipping partner, married Elizabeth Roosevelt. Maternal grandfather of Robert Cogdell Gilchrist.

Elizabeth Roosevelt (1762-1819)
From her uncle, the early land developer, John Thurman (1730-1809), she inherited thousands of Adirondack acres. Maternal grandmother of Robert Cogdell Gilchrist.

Mary Gilchrist (1797-1867)
Daughter of Elizabeth Roosevelt and Robert A. Gilchrist. Mother of Robert Cogdell Gilchrist.

Robert Budd Gilchrist (1796-1856)
Oldest son of Adam Gilchrist of Charleston. Attorney and federal judge who married his first cousin, Mary Gilchrist. Father of Robert Cogdell Gilchrist.

Robert Gilchrist of The Glen (1795-1869)
Oldest son of Elizabeth Roosevelt and Robert A. Gilchrist. Businessman and attorney. Brother of Mary Gilchrist and uncle to Robert Cogdell Gilchrist.

Mary Augusta Gibbes (1844-1913)
"Gussie" is the wife of Robert Cogdell Gilchrist, and descendant of Charleston's Gibbes and Roper families.

GILCHRIST FAMILY TREE

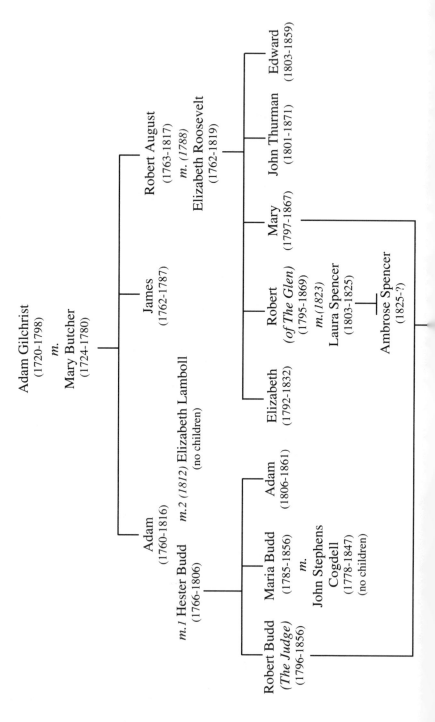

Adam Gilchrist
(1720-1798)

m.

Mary Butcher
(1724-1780)

Adam
(1760-1816)

m.1 Hester Budd
(1766-1806)

m.2 (1812) Elizabeth Lamboll
(no children)

James
(1762-1787)

Robert August
(1763-1817)

m. (1788)

Elizabeth Roosevelt
(1762-1819)

Robert Budd
(*The Judge*)
(1796-1856)

Maria Budd
(1785-1856)

m.

John Stephens
Cogdell
(1778-1847)
(no children)

Adam
(1806-1861)

Elizabeth
(1792-1832)

Robert
(*of The Glen*)
(1795-1869)

m.(1823)

Laura Spencer
(1803-1825)

Mary
(1797-1867)

John Thurman
(1801-1871)

Edward
(1803-1859)

Ambrose Spencer
(1825-?)

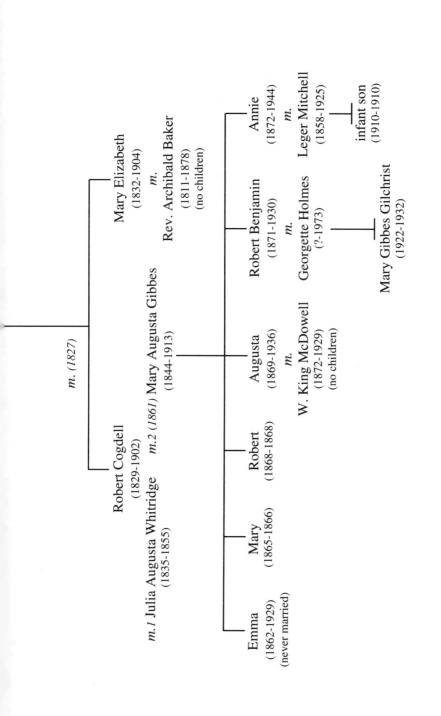

m. (1827)

Robert Cogdell
(1829-1902)

Mary Elizabeth
(1832-1904)
m.
Rev. Archibald Baker
(1811-1878)
(no children)

m.1 Julia Augusta Whitridge   m.2 (1861) Mary Augusta Gibbes
(1835-1855)   (1844-1913)

Emma
(1862-1929)
(never married)

Mary
(1865-1866)

Robert
(1868-1868)

Augusta
(1869-1936)
m.
W. King McDowell
(1872-1929)
(no children)

Robert Benjamin
(1871-1930)
m.
Georgette Holmes
(?-1973)

Annie
(1872-1944)
m.
Leger Mitchell
(1858-1925)

Mary Gibbes Gilchrist
(1922-1932)

infant son
(1910-1910)

CHAPTER ONE

Kissing Cousins

Long before there was an Ellis Island to process immigrants, Adam Gilchrist and his wife, Mary Butcher, left their home in Edinburgh and sailed to the colonies for a new life. The year was 1750. Her father was a silversmith in England, and among the possessions they brought were a silver tankard, some silver spoons, and a small marble clock. They settled in New York where in just three years, three sons were born.

By the time the colonies declared their independence, their sons were grown and the oldest, Adam, was sent to Charleston as a lieutenant in Colonel William Washington's Regiment. He stayed on, married a doctor's daughter, Hester Budd, and went into the shipping business. During the years the great masted ships plied their trade on the Atlantic highway, his several vessels sailed directly between Charleston and Liverpool.

Adam succeeded in business, was a founder of the Charleston Chamber of Commerce, and eventually became president of the U.S. Bank in Charleston. Surviving one war, he was caught up in a second war for independence when the British began seizing his ships. Those losses, in what was called the War of 1812, forced him into bankruptcy. After the death of his first wife, Hester, Adam took a second wife, the wealthy Elizabeth Lamboll. With his second wife's money, he was able to start over. His business partner and youngest brother, Robert, was not so fortunate.

Robert August Gilchrist had married Elizabeth Roosevelt at Trinity Church in New York City on July 16, 1787. As
the New York based partner of the brother's shipping firm,
his wealth grew and the family lived in luxury. But the War
of 1812 cost him his fortune, too, as the British continued
seizing ships. To cancel his debts he turned his property
over to creditors and retired, broken in spirit, to his wife's
lands in the Adirondacks. He died shortly afterwards and
was buried in a small cemetery in the Adirondack hamlet of
Wevertown, New York.

Both of these brothers who had served in the Revolutionary War would be the grandfathers of a Civil War officer who inherited their fighting spirit.

The middle brother, James, studied medicine and
became a surgeon in the Privateers, the government's first
navy. He never married, traveled extensively, and brought
back fine china and exotic gifts such as ginger from India.
Sent to investigate the health of the citizens of Georgetown
during a summer of extended sickness, he contracted country fever and died there in 1787.

Adam's oldest son, Robert Budd Gilchrist, was a handsome young lawyer who began travelling north each summer
after he passed the bar in 1818. The journey by vessel,
stagecoach and canal boat was a hardship in the 1820s, but
summer in the Great Northern Wilderness—not yet named
Adirondacks—was preferable to the humid weather of a
Charleston summer. He was also courting his first cousin,
Mary Gilchrist, daughter of Robert August Gilchrist and
Elizabeth Roosevelt.

The typical keepsakes exchanged between couples at
that time were miniature portraits done in watercolor on
ivory. At the Gibbes Museum of Art in Charleston there is a
miniature done by the artist Charles Fraser, of Robert Budd
Gilchrist, perhaps at Mary's request.

Mary's miniature portrait can also be found at the
Gibbes Museum of Art although the artist is unidentified. It
shows her in a dress with its Empire waistline in the style of

the 1820s, topped with a crisp white ruff of a collar called a 'betsy.' She was a slim and pretty young woman, with fine features and dark hair parted in the middle with a topknot or bun held in place with braids.

They were an attractive couple. He described as, "Of extremely handsome personal appearance . . . enhanced by prematurely snow-white, silvery hair combined with a delicate, youthful expression. These attractions were perfected by exquisite old world manners that proceeded from an honest, kindly heart. No wonder then that he drew to himself and won the hearts of his fellow men." After a seven year courtship, he won Mary.

At a time when wealth was kept within family alliances, it was not uncommon for first cousins to marry. Robert Budd Gilchrist and his first cousin Mary Gilchrist were wed in Albany, New York on September 20, 1827, merging both families as well as the china dinner sets brought back from their uncle's travels.

They moved to their first home on Church Street in Charleston, one of the largest, richest and most beautiful of cities by the beginning of the 19th century. Rice, indigo, and slaves created Charleston's wealth. During the last century of the large sailing ships, the city grew to become an important seaport. Its waterfront, with a high seawall built to guard the harbor, was called the Battery, and was the first seaside boardwalk in the country. The fashionable promenade was (and is) a favorite place to stroll—to look out at the water—at Fort Sumter—to view the surrounding islands that once defended the city from invasion.

The men of the rice plantations often had townhouses in the city, and to showcase their owners' wealth, the houses in the 19th century became greater and taller. It was a city of cobbled streets, narrow alleys, spacious white antebellum homes overlooking the Battery, Federal brick homes, and always the gallery or piazza to catch the sea breeze. Pastel colored stucco homes looked out over the water from East Bay Street where the couple moved next.

The beautiful Charleston homes and their manicured

Judge Robert Budd Gilchrist, father of Robert C. Gilchrist.
Miniature watercolor in ivory by Charles Fraser.

Mary Gilchrist, mother of Robert C. Gilchrist and wife of
Robert Budd Gilchrist. Miniature watercolor on ivory, artist
unknown.

gardens can still be glimpsed today through wrought iron gates set in brick walls. While early settlers sought to create a life and home like those they remembered in England, they were forced to make certain concessions because of the subtropical climate as well as the influence of settlers from Barbados. The single house, the width of one room, with the house turning its shoulder to the street to insure privacy, had its long open piazza at one side to catch the breeze and was protected by a door on the street side. A double house was similarly designed but was two rooms wide.

Flowers bloom almost year round; sea grasses, daffodils and pansies still abound during the mild winters. Spring alone is a reason for living there to see and smell the roses, magnolias, azaleas, and wisteria. Even hot summers have oleander, crepe myrtle and althea.

It had been very different in the Adirondacks when Mary and her family lived there, after her father lost his fortune in the War of 1812. The family had lived rather plainly in a simple frame house. An unknown author wrote in the family journal:

> ". . . misfortune followed them even into the mountain wilds. One inclement winter night a pedlar [sic] came to the door for shelter. He was fed, then conducted by their hired man to a comfortable shed room where he was lodged for the night. In the wee small hours when the family was wrapped in slumber they were awakened by finding their house enveloped in flames. Out into the open they hurried but half clad where a gale was blowing and a heavy snowstorm was falling, but there was no time to lose. The house was quickly consumed leaving not a stick upon another. The clock was saved by being hastily thrown out of a second story window into a snowbank, and the next day recovered intact. As the pedlar had mysteriously disappeared, never to be seen again, it was always supposed that he had first robbed his benefactors, then covered up his dastardly deed by firing the dwelling when he decamped."

When Mary married and moved to Charleston she brought the family clock that had been carried from Scotland and saved in the Adirondack fire. Described as not more than twelve inches high, the clock was supported by marble pillars, with a free-swinging pendulum and the maker's name on the face.

Fires continually threatened the citizens of Charleston in the crowded sections of wooden homes. The city survived numerous fires including the earlier fire of 1740. The colonial assembly had declared houses be built of brick, but this was largely ignored.

In 1838, a news reporter wrote, "Square after square was demolished with a speed almost electrical." The fire began in a wooden two-story house at the corner of King and Beresford Streets, "and was not extinguished until it reached the water's edge on Cooper River. . . . The immense distress from the unfortunate families who have been thrown out of homes and even a shelter for some of them is beyond description." The reporter estimated some twelve to fifteen hundred were homeless from the fire.

When Mary and Robert Budd Gilchrist's East Bay Street home caught fire, the family clock was saved again by being put in a copper coal scuttle, along with a likeness of Mary's husband. It was left there in a marsh lot opposite the house until the next morning when they moved to the new suburb of Mazyckboro. The peninsular city expanded northward during the antebellum period to the higher ground that had once been Alexander Mazyck's pasture, and Mary and her husband lived there until another home on East Bay Street could be built.

A year after the tragic fire of 1838, President Van Buren appointed Robert Budd Gilchrist to the lifetime position of federal judge. Genial and sociable, he enjoyed the friendship of other prominent Charlestonians as a Captain in The Washington Light Infantry, as President of the St. Cecelia Society, and as President of a Literary Club which met at members' homes to read and discuss papers. Agitation over states' rights and slavery grew as anti-slavery tracts were mailed to Charleston, and a mob tried to seize the mails. Like James Louis Petigru, the famous antebellum lawyer, Judge Gilchrist was a Unionist living in the 'cradle of secession,' holding unpopular political views, and married to a Yankee! But, like Petigru, he was respected in spite of his views.

The buying and selling of slaves continued in the area bound by Meeting and Broad Streets and Queen and East Bay, close to the Judge's home. He believed slavery was not a divine institution; all humans should be free.

Yet he would read advertisements in *The Charleston Courier*, "Woman for Sale - an elderly Woman about 40 years old, of warranted character, good cook, washer, ironer, and house servant, sold for no fault." Another read, ". . . at the mart on East Bay, at 11 o'clock, at the risk of the former owner, a Negro Woman named Bess, and her child Heather. The woman Bess having proved unsound. Conditions cash. Purchaser to pay for bill of sale."

Not only didn't the North understand their 'peculiar institution,' the South felt the North was developing its manufacturing at their expense. The Tariff of 1828, known as the Tariff of Abominations, was followed by the Tariff of 1832 which cut some rates, but still angered the South. They viewed these taxes on imports as protecting New England industries and feared retaliation on the southern exports of tobacco, cotton and rice.

John Calhoun authored the Southern response, declaring a state's right to nullify federal laws it viewed as unconstitutional. He resigned the vice-presidency to become South Carolina's Senator to the U.S. Congress and argue the South's interests. Feeling there was no relief from the federal government, a South Carolina State convention adopted an Ordinance of Nullification declaring the Tariffs of 1828 and 1832 'null and void' within the state.

Amid the passions of nullification in Charleston, the first child of Judge Robert Budd and Mary Gilchrist was born on June 2, 1829, and named Robert Cogdell Gilchrist.

There were other events occurring in the nation which

would also shape their young child's future. Elsewhere in the country the Baltimore and Ohio Railroad, in 1830, tried out the first American-built locomotive, the "Tom Thumb," when it raced against a horse. The horse won, but the 'iron horse' was to be the future.

The following year the first passenger train in this country to be drawn by a steam locomotive made its inaugural run between Albany and Schenectady, New York. The little engine was not quite twelve feet long, and the attached cars looked like stagecoaches. A crowd turned out for the grand occasion and railroad fever seized the country.

President Andrew Jackson had warned that disunity was treason and by 1833 Congress passed the Force Act authorizing military action to uphold federal law. Yet the same Congress passed the Compromise Tariff of 1833 enabling South Carolina to withdraw its Ordinance of Nullification.

Rail transportation would always interest this child of Mary and the Judge. That and bridging the differences between his mother's North and his father's South.

Throughout the confident 19th century and into the next, the small marble clock saved in the fire would keep the time—times of sweeping change for the country, and for Robert Cogdell Gilchrist.

CHAPTER TWO

Growing Up in Charleston

Growing up in Charleston, the Judge's son could hear the nearby bells of St. Michael's Episcopal Church faithfully marking the time at the corner of Meeting and Broad Streets, and hear the horse-drawn wagons rumbling along the cobblestone streets of the city. In school he probably heard the traditional geography lesson that taught that the Ashley and Cooper Rivers met in Charleston, leading to the Atlantic Ocean.

In the 1830's, young Robert was growing up on East Bay Street, still one of the most fashionable addresses. It is easy to imagine him playing in the park below at Oyster Point, or walking the seawall promenade guarded by a white-turbaned 'mauma,' or perhaps by Billy Green, the young slave his father hired to watch over his boy. Slaves in antebellum Charleston could hire themselves out, pay their owner a certain amount, and keep the rest. Billy Green came to the Judge when he learned his master intended to sell him. Aware of his son's attachment to Billy, Judge Gilchrist, although opposed to slavery, bought his only slave. Billy repaid with loyalty until he died, and was a bodyguard to his young master throughout the Civil War, protecting the entire family from the enemy during Sherman's raid in Cheraw, South Carolina.

With family mentors who were talented and successful businessmen, the boy did indeed seem predestined for great

11

Photograph by Wes Pelkey

St. Michael's Church. J. S. Cogdell and his wife, Maria, are buried here.

East Bay Street, Charleston, where Robert Cogdell Gilchrist grew up.

things. His father's law partner was John Stevens Cogdell, a man of many talents. Cogdell painted and sculpted, and had wanted to do so professionally, but his friend and fellow artist, Washington Allston, advised him, "Do not let it tempt you to give up a certainty for an uncertainty. . . . If by making the art your profession you are to depend on it as the means of support for yourself and family, I cannot but think you look to a very precarious source."

Taking Allston's advice, he followed an active legal and business career. But even with art as an avocation only, he is recognized as South Carolina's first sculptor. He found time to serve in the State Assembly and, in 1832, was elected President of the Bank of South Carolina.

John Stevens Cogdell married his law partner's sister, Maria Budd Gilchrist. The devoted couple, without children of their own, had a namesake in the Judge's son, young Robert Cogdell Gilchrist, and made room in their lives for their precocious nephew. In all likelihood, John Stevens Cogdell was the first art teacher of the gifted child.

His parents commissioned the artist George Cooke to paint a double portrait of Robert and his younger sister, Mary Elizabeth, when he was seven. They were pretty and privileged children, smiling and alert as they sat for the artist who had Robert hold one of his father's law books and a pencil where he'd drawn a horse in the book.

As a child he painted landscapes and Charleston's *Courier* of November 16, 1843, commented that, "William Tell's Chapel is from the pencil of a very young artist who has contributed before to the Gallery, and who certainly exhibits, even this early, the dawn of a progressing talent for the fine arts, which does not often display itself at as early a period of eleven years of age!" The Gibbes Museum of Art holds two of his landscapes.

A friend said of Gilchrist, "His art instincts were strong, and he displayed far more than a simple taste for mechanics . . .", apparently referring to Gilchrist at age fourteen winning a prominent prize at the Carolina Institute Fair for making, unaided, a model of a steam engine.

John Stevens Cogdell, 1778-1847. Miniature watercolor in
ivory by Charles Fraser.

Courtesy of the Gibbes Museum of Art

Robert and Elizabeth Gilchrist, 1836. Oil on canvas by
George Cooke.

Courtesy of the Gibbes Museum of Art
Oil on canvas painted by Robert Cogdell Gilchrist.

Winning admission to the College of Charleston required candidates to be able to translate works in both
Greek and Latin. Each day's classes began with Scripture
reading and prayer, and each student was to take his turn
at exercises in elocution, committing to memory pieces
approved by the faculty. Inspiring speeches made to men he
later commanded may have come from these early lessons.

About the time Gilchrist graduated from the College of
Charleston in 1849, the same artist who painted him as a
child, did another portrait. He was then a handsome man
with serious eyes, sensitive full mouth, a widow's peak of
dark hair above a high forehead, and facial 'mutton chops'
which made him appear older than his twenty years.

Paul Hamilton Hayne, a college friend, described him
as quiet and introspective. He was seen as more reserved
than his genial father, yet they enjoyed a close and affectionate relationship. In a letter to Robert's sister when she
was at school in Connecticut, their father pokes fun at the
seriousness which his son displayed as a marching cadet.

"Our celebration of the fourth of July passed off without any accident occurring to mar the joys and festivities of the day. The troops as usual assembled at an early hour in the morning and exhibited themselves to the admiring gaze of the fair daughters of Carolina. I say 'fair' for you know it is customary to compliment ladies and particularly young ladies with the epithet of fair however much their complexions may be embarrassed by the rays of a summer sun."

"Among the valiant heroes was to be seen that youthful and patriotic corps, the College Cadets, marching as if the fate of the nation hung on the precision of their movements and their breasts swelling with all that martial ardor which animated the bosom of an Alexander, a Caesar, a Bonaparte, a Wellington and a long list of military characters to deeds of heroic daring."

"And foremost among the worthies of the College Cadets was to be found that distinguished young officer, R.C.G., who nobly perspired on that day in the service of his country. But I will not dwell any longer on this interesting theme, and will leave to your imagination to fill up the picture which I might sketch of processing orations, fireworks, etc. Your brother spent the evening on the Battery with the Ingrahams and some others of the rising generations."

The portrait of the young cadet gets further brushstrokes from his college friend Hayne who said of him, "There was a youth of apparently frail physique, of quiet and retired manners, in whom, although he achieved no special scholastic distinction in the orthodox curriculum, his associates recognized certain peculiar talents. . . . We all believed that our friend, Robert C. Gilchrist, would secure fame and fortune as a painter or inventor, perhaps as both. I observed upon his face that strange, introspective look which strikes one in the portraits of Watt and Stephenson."

At the time of his college graduation in 1849, Gilchrist joined the Washington Light Infantry as his father had. The company had been organized in 1807 and named for the country's first President. It served as honor guard when Lafayette visited Charleston in 1824 and saw service in the Mexican War. Gilchrist would rejoin it in later life and become its commander.

After college he studied law under the well-known lawyer, James Louis Petigru, a Unionist like his father. Petigru had moved to a new office building, designed to resemble a Greek temple, where he occupied a large room on the second floor. The first floor held his partner's office, and a room for students and law clerks. Here Gilchrist studied for the bar, passing it in 1850, the same year the Compromise of 1850 held the Union together for another ten years.

He practiced law in that decade and was involved in his mother's church and a number of civic activities. He initiated the idea of a Y.M.C.A. being established in Charleston, although the raised funds were lost during the war.

In other parts of the country people were reading and reacting to *Uncle Tom's Cabin*. The 1852 book popularized the abolition movement, sold 300,000 copies within a year, and was eventually produced as a play. Passions were further inflamed in the spring of 1854 as *The New York Times* reported an "ineradicable hatred" had been created by the passage of the Kansas-Nebraska Act. The law let settlers of the territories decide for themselves whether to be a free or slave state and the resulting violence within 'bleeding Kansas' foreshadowed the coming war between the states.

Robert's parents were in upstate New York in the summer of 1854 hoping the mineral waters at Sharon Springs would help the ailing Judge. He wrote to his son:

> "I have received my dear son your affectionate letter of the 23rd instant and am highly satisfied that you and my sister still experience your accustomed health, although that scourge of our city has made its appearance. . . . On this point however great may be my anxiety I leave your movements to the exercise of your own judgment, trusting at the same time that you will exhibit all that prudence which you have promised me."

He reminded his son that:

> "Your mother requests your aunt to attend to the picking of the red peppers and have them pounded or ground for use,"

and added she was:

> "still suffering from dyspepsia, though it is not as bad as it was."

As for his own health, his father wrote:

> "I shall leave this place with sincere regret, for here I have regained a portion of the health which I have lost . . . and if I possessed the poetic fervor of our friend Mr. Yeardon, I should sing its praises in verse, but as I am denied the possession of that talent I must proclaim its excellencies in plain prose instead of immortal song—which I do by saying that I would recommend it to every invalid."

Two close relationships ended for Robert in that decade. Little is known of his first wife, Julia Whitridge, who died in 1855. His father died a year later. Apparently finding comfort in his mother's Presbyterian church, he became Sunday School Superintendent. In 1859 he turned thirty, a widower living at 245 East Bay Street with a law office at 13 Chalmers Street. The cobblestones of Chalmers Street are still there, but a bank parking lot today replaces the building.

Gilchrist's Christmas letter to the church teachers in 1859 reveals his sense of responsibility, and perhaps a bit of righteousness, as he wrote in the eloquent prose of the day: ". . . it behooves us to be up and doing our work diligently. . . . Would I be pardoned if I was occasionally two or five minutes behind the time. And yet, when the week closes, I am as wearied, and the Sabbath morning finds my eyelids as heavy as any of the teachers. Once, when I was two minutes late by *his* watch, a teacher took me to task for it. Friend! why should not the rule work both ways. Do you not know that your scholars hold you to as strict an account as you do me? Often have my lips been closed, when urging a more punctual attendance on the part of the children, by their answer: 'Why sir, I am in school before my teacher.' Punctuality consists in being present at the very moment the exercises commence."

He went on to plead for their support and an improvement in communication between teachers and officers. He specifically urged their attendance at the next Teacher's meeting.

Whether the teachers came and the children and teachers were more punctual after that, the new year of 1860 presented greater problems than Sunday School attendance to Gilchrist.

With passions rising over slavery and its extension to the western territories, the Gilchrist family was aware that travel north might soon be impossible. Gilchrist served as a witness to a legal paper stating his Adirondack uncle, Robert Gilchrist of The Glen, would collect land rents and manage property Robert's mother and her two brothers owned in the northern mountains.

Not only were families divided by questions of secession, the slavery issue split the Democratic party's national convention at Charleston. Delegates from eight Southern states, including South Carolina, left the convention and chose John C. Breckinridge as their candidate. Northern Democrats nominated Stephen Douglas.

When Lincoln won the Republican nomination, South Carolinians vowed to secede if he was elected. Within days after Lincoln's victory, the state legislature voted to have a convention to consider secession.

The pealing of church bells and din of saluting guns outside Charleston's South Carolina Institute Hall on December 20, 1860, signaled the state's vote for independence from the Union.

Robert Cogdell Gilchrist, born of a Yankee mother and a Charleston father, would have to make a choice.

CHAPTER THREE

War Comes

Robert Cogdell Gilchrist was not the only Southerner who had to choose between region and country. The South's favorite general, Robert E. Lee, was first asked to lead the Union troops. He had earlier freed his slaves and was opposed to secession, but loyalty to his native Virginia led him to join the Confederate cause.

The lawyer, James Petigru, was another who opposed secession yet stayed in the South. He wrote, "I would not part from my sisters, my friends, and all who depend upon me." A friend of Gilchrist's, Major David Ramsey, died fighting for the South, yet some questioned his loyalty because he was unsympathetic to the Confederate cause. Gilchrist defended Ramsey in a letter to Paul Hamilton Hayne and said, "We were both Union men and were in full accord as to our opinion of secession. But when the fatal die was cast I thought it my duty to go with my state right or wrong and by fighting for her endeavor to right her."

That sense of duty caused Gilchrist to stay in Charleston and help recruit the Zouave cadets with Captain C.E. Chichester. They were one of 28 Charleston companies of part-time soldiers, militia units that made up what Southern army existed in the city. The Charleston Zouaves were the first to march to the headquarters of Governor Pickens to volunteer their services upon news of secession.

The name Zouave was used by a number of volunteer

regiments on both sides who adopted the dress and drill of the French infantry composed of Algerians. These Algerians wore colorful uniforms of baggy trousers, short open-front jackets and tasseled caps, and were admired for their very quick and spirited drills.

Gilchrist's Zouaves were to have fancy uniforms of a blue jacket, scarlet pants and scarlet cap, but eventually showed up in serviceable, gray cloth for their first dress parade in early December 1860. The cadets were supposedly made up of teetotallers, as was, in all likelihood, the young man raised by his religiously strict mother. High standards were set for enlisting in his Zouaves.

A recruiting paper read, "Any person of Moral Character and Gentlemanly deportment, and who is 17 years old and measures 5 feet 4 inches in height may become an active member."

There was a payment of $5 a year to these part-time militiamen, and there were rules which included no drinking in uniform, no patronage of saloons, no gambling, and cadets were forbidden to enter a house of 'ill-fame.'

The Zouave cadets supported the Citadel cadets in firing on the steamer, 'Star of the West,' sent to reinforce Union forces at Fort Sumter at the beginning of 1861. Pierre Gustave Toutant DeBeauregard arrived that March to take command of Charleston and set about to improve the city's defenses and take Fort Sumter. He eventually became one of the eight full generals of the Confederacy.

Beauregard ordered the attack on Fort Sumter on April 12th, 1861. Gilchrist was on duty on Sullivan's Island during the bombardment. From the rooftops of the mansions along the Battery and East Bay Street where Gilchrist had grown up, the people of Charleston watched the shelling and cheered the Confederacy. Two days later, Union forces surrendered.

In April 1861, renowned diarist Mary Boykin Chesnut was in Charleston and writing in her diary: "In the afternoon Mrs. Preston, Mrs. Joe Heyward and I drove around the Battery. We were in an open carriage. What a changed

Post-Courier, Charleston

Zouave Cadets guarding Castle Pinckney, 1861.

Courtesy *Post-Courier*, Charleston

Charlestonians watch the shelling of Fort Sumter from their rooftops.

scene! The very liveliest crowd I think I ever saw. Everyone talking at once, all glasses still turned on the grim old Fort."

She stayed at the Mills House and described the "noise of drums, tramp of marching regiments all day long, rattling of artillery wagons, bands of music, friends from every quarter coming in. We ought to be miserable and anxious, and yet these are pleasant days. Perhaps we are unnaturally exhilarated and excited."

At the beginning of the war the Charleston *Courier* tried to check the enthusiasm of some by saying, "A great proportion of our sick soldiers are boys. The practice of permitting boys to enlist in the army for active service cannot be too strongly condemned." On the Union side some one thousand recruits were under fifteen years of age.

Meanwhile, emotions other than the fever of war animated Robert Gilchrist's life in 1861. Not always on duty, he began courting Mary Augusta Gibbes with carriage rides. "If the weather permits, will Miss Augusta take a ride with me this afternoon at 6 o'clock?"

The perfect writing that won him first prize for penmanship at the South Carolina Institute in 1850, was now seen on his calling cards.

It was a year for change for Gilchrist and the country. In Charleston a new city railway was incorporated which planned to use horsedrawn cars—and there was a new way to bury the dead. Mary Boykin Chesnut wrote, "Mrs. Capers and Mrs. Tom Middleton came for me and we drove to Magnolia Cemetery to see the Vanderhorst way of burying the dead. One is embalmed, kept life-like by some process, dressed as usual, can be seen through a glass case. I did not look. How can anyone? . . . It was hard to shake off the blues after this graveyard business."

The luxury of that kind of burial was denied those who fell in the first battle of Bull Run that July. Early in the war both sides looked on the fighting as a spectacle—a sporting event. The citizens of Washington took their carriages out to picnic and watch the Union army defeat Johnny Reb. Instead the northern retreat became a panic-stricken flight.

Captured prisoners from Bull Run were taken to Castle Pinckney to be guarded by Gilchrist's Zouave cadets. Thirty officers and one hundred privates of the Union Army were confined in Castle Pinckney.

Commander Chichester's wife later wrote "A Lady's Experience Inside the Forts in Charleston Harbor During the War." She described a breakfast call for the men that consisted of "fried bacon, corn bread and molasses, and a tin cup full of steaming hot coffee. . . ." When an unexpected visit came from General Ripley, she was the hostess who wrote, "Fortunately the colored boy had been sent out that day at low water to rake up a good supply of fresh oysters which we had raw and stewed with hot coffee, hot biscuits, good butter, etc."

The illusion that secession would not bring war, was followed by another illusion—that the war would be short. Social life in Charleston went on as it always had before the blockade strangled the city. Gala parties continued, but now soldiers going to war moved up their wedding days.

Gussie, the eldest daughter of Anne and Benjamin Gibbes, turned seventeen only a week before her marriage to Robert Cogdell Gilchrist, who was thirty-two years old. In a letter, her mother, Anne Roper Gibbes, described the ceremony joining the two well-connected families of Charleston in 1861.

"My Dear Sue,

Augusta informed you why her wedding day was anticipated. I was quite startled when it was first proposed to me, and I was obliged to make great exertions to complete my preparations for the 15th Oct. instead of the 6th Nov.

Gussie wore a double skirt of organdie, the lower had three frills, the upper was looped up with bows of ribbon, a veil of tulle confined to the head by a wreath of myrtle flowers reached to the hem of her skirt, gloves trimmed with a deep quilling of tulle. I will not bid you make allowance for maternal vanity, but will only say the general voice was 'how lovely.' She looked

like a beautiful vision. Several remarked to me, 'how
sweetly Gussie looks.'

They issued 400 invitations, but a number of un-
invited guests also filled the church, which was bril-
liantly lit up. Dr. Smyth was seated in a large chair
near the pulpit, radiant with smiles. He rose as I
entered with Richard, followed by the bridal party,
last of all Robert and Augusta. A small company of
thirty-five immediate relations and friends adjourned
to my house to supper.''

The reception was held at 4 John Street, around the
corner from the Second Presbyterian Church. The beautiful
three-storied home is believed to have been built by Gabriel
Manigault. Inside the main foyer where Gussie's guests
entered, there is still some of the original wallpaper painted
to look like marble. Wedding guests stood in the living
room before the carved mantle depicting an angel leading a
Roman chariot and soldiers into battle. The high-ceilinged
dining room on the other side of the double house could
easily hold the thirty-five guests.

Gilchrist's bride, Mary Augusta Gibbes, came from a
prominent family. She was a great-granddaughter of the
Robert Gibbes who had been governor when South Carolina
was a proprietory colony. A number of other relatives were
also leading citizens, such as: Dr. Robert Gibbes, South
Carolina's Surgeon General; Professor Lewis Gibbes of the
College of Charleston; and Gussie's cousin, James Shoolbred Gibbes, who left to Charleston a legacy for building
the Gibbes Museum of Art. Paul Hamilton Hayne, poet and
aristocrat, and Robert's college friend, may have been one
of the guests among the invited relatives and friends at 4
John Street.

While a semblance of normal life was maintained,
hardships continued to be documented by Mrs. Chesnut. In
October, her diary entry read, "Thank God for pine knots!
Gas and candles and oil are all disappearing in the Confederacy."

In December 1861, there was a devastating fire that lit

Photograph by Wes Pelkey

Second Presbyterian Church where Gilchrist was married.

Photograph by Patricia Jordan

4 John Street, the home of Gilchrist's wife, Gussie, and the site of their wedding reception.

up the city short on candles. She wrote, "Charleston is in flames, one part of the city utterly destroyed. On the night of the eleventh, we had here a furious windstorm. We rather enjoyed it, in the interest of the Yankee Fleet outside of the Bar there." Her next day's entry reveals, "More news of the Charleston fire. Carolina Institute, where secession was signed, burned down, and so did Mr. Petigru's house. . . . The fire appeared simultaneously in several places."

More change and more problems came to the South in 1862 as term-expired men refused to enlist, and spring meant farmer soldiers went home to plant a crop and failed to return. Confederate armies were shrinking. In May, the Confederate Congress passed an act disbanding the state militia and requiring all males over eighteen to volunteer for three years of war.

Gilchrist raised the Gist Guards artillery and became 1st Lieutenant under Captain C.E. Chichester. By June he was on James Island writing to Gussie. Sent to "Mrs. R.C. Gilchrist, St. Georges Post Office, S.C. Railroad, S.C.," his return address read, "Soldier's letter, Lt. R.C. Gilchrist, Gist Guard, Earthworks, James Island." He had been to see her and forgot keys he needed. He wrote:

> "My darling Gussie,
> I have just received the bundle containing the box of keys. . . . I had however succeeded yesterday in picking my trunk and so ceased to be inconvenienced by the want of it, and was chiefly anxious to get your dear letter. . . . In my opinion my visit to you was very cheaply purchased by the temporary inconvenience of not being able to get into my trunk, and most willingly would I seal it up hermetically, for the pleasure of being able to visit you once more. Next time I make such a trip, I don't intend to be cut short as I was last time, but will make my arrangements to spend the whole night with you and see something of your mode of living at Georges."

His letter dated June 20, 1862 was just after the battle of Secessionville on James Island. Like protective arms,

Sullivan and James Islands encompassed the harbor in an embracing curve. Control of either island would enable the North to fire on Charleston. In the early hours of June 16th, pickets warned the Secessionville Fort they'd been overrun by advancing Yankees.

The fighting at times was hand to hand as defenders of the fort used bayonets, and their rifles as clubs. The marsh and pluff mud reduced the attackers' ability to make formations so that the assault was piecemeal and ineffective. Within a few hours almost nine hundred men were killed, wounded or captured in a bitter fight before the Yankees retreated.

Reserved in dealing with others, a warmer Lt. Gilchrist wrote to his child bride,

> ". . . But darling, you must not be so anxious about me. I can assure you I am very well in health and comfortably located, and should anything ever be the matter with me I will certainly let you know it. Therefore when you do not hear from me, lay it to the mail or anything else that will not cause anxiety. . . . I have strong hopes of my being able to return home before the summer is over. . . ."

Instead, he was sent to Morris Island in July to assist in building Battery Wagner.

CHAPTER FOUR

Defending Charleston

It was during 1862 that Battery Wagner was slowly transformed into a fort of earthworks. Mrs. Chesnut wrote, "Anne Hampton came to tell us the latest news that we . . . are fortifying Morris Island; and she says: 'If the enemy will be so kind as to wait, we well be ready for them in two months.'"

Fighting didn't wait in other places—New Orleans had been captured in April. In Tennessee, Confederate General A.S. Johnston was killed in the slaughter at Shiloh and Beauregard assumed command. Gunboat warfare continued off Virginia's coastline as the ironclads *Monitor* and *Merrimack* dueled—each claiming victory, and forever changing the way navies would fight.

For Gilchrist the work went on, fortifying Wagner on Morris Island. In a letter to Gussie he said:

> "I would write oftener than twice a week, but I have so little to write about. One day passes just like every other and if I fill my letters with nothing but expressions of affection, although true, I fear you will get tired of reading them.
>
> "Your letters are indeed a comfort to me and almost reconcile me to being separated from you. Stop! That is saying too much for nothing can do so. But indeed they are a great comfort to me, as your own heart tells you."

"We have very little sickness now, two cases of
fever in the company. I hope you will be careful, in all
your excursions, to do nothing that will tax your
strength. Remember dearest that you are the guard-
ian of one, only less dear to me than you are, and
great would be my disappointment if anything should
happen to you, or it."

"In each and every letter let me know how you
are getting on. You know how much interested I am. I
am sorry you suffer so much from the heat."

He suggested she leave the window open at the foot of the
bed and worried,

". . . if you don't obtain and enjoy your night's rest,
you will indeed melt away to a shadow."

The weather turned cooler at summer's end and on
October 27, 1862, their first daughter, Emma, was born.

Meanwhile Charleston remained the symbol of resistance. Labeled the 'cradle of Secession' and 'the nursery of
treason and rebellion,' Union military felt proud Charleston
must be taken and humbled.

Gilchrist described the strategic importance of Morris
Island: "Skirting along ship channel, the main entrance
into Charleston Harbor, and thus commanding the only
approach for large vessels to the city, is Morris Island—
forever prominent in the history of the United States. . . ."

In command of the city's defenses, Beauregard thought
the enemy would advance over James Island and so removed
the slave laborers from Morris Island to strengthen fortifications elsewhere. Gilchrist's Gist Guard and Matthews'
Artillery were left to finish the half-completed battery. Confederate General Roswell Ripley, a Northerner by birth, was
credited with what defenses were built among the sand hills
at the southern end of Morris.

The crescent-shaped island was then not quite four
miles long and twenty-five hundred yards at its widest,
being no more than two feet above sea level. Only four

Courtesy of *Post-Courier*
Confederate mortar battery on Morris Island.

hundred yards of inlet separated it from Folly Island and
Yankee encroachments. The engineer Beauregard was busy
fortifying the city; Union troops gained, undiscovered, a
foothold on Folly Island just south of Morris Island.

Under the cover of sand hills and a heavy growth of
scrubby trees, the Union troops were able to secretly place a
battery of forty-seven pieces of artillery, shelters and maga-
zines on Folly Island, even though they were "almost within
speaking distance of Confederate pickets." At night the
Union infantry and engineers quietly built their gun posi-
tions, leaving before each dawn.

This foothold, such a strategic point, caused later
Southern recriminations. Questioned as to why the Confederates hadn't cleared the trees that hid Yankee movements
and obscured the view from Morris, Beauregard said he
never believed an attack would be launched from there.

Three miles from the southern end of Morris Island,
and three-fourths of a mile from its northern end, Battery
Wagner stretched across a narrow section of land, its guns

Courtesy *Post Courier*
U.S. troops assault Battery Wagner, July 18, 1863.

protecting Fort Sumter, which was being held by the Confederates. There was an enclosed parade ground of about an acre. The fort was an enclosed earth-work that contained a bomb-proof magazine twenty-by-twenty feet, and a shelter that measured thirty by one hundred and thirty feet where nine hundred men could be wedged in.

Gilchrist later wrote, "In fact, not more than three hundred could, or ever did, obtain shelter in it at one time." One third of the fort was used as a hospital, further reducing available space.

A force of 12,000 Union men, including naval power, was sent to take Morris Island. On July 10, 1863, the Union's General Quincy A. Gilmore was ready to assault Morris Island from Folly and opened fire across the narrow inlet. Two thousand Yankee troops crossing in rowboats stormed ashore, supported by fire from four Navy monitors. Within musket range of Fort Wagner this first attack halted, with the Union counting fifteen dead and ninety-one wounded. Confederate losses were higher—two hundred ninety-four killed, wounded or captured.

The next day losses were reversed when four companies of Union men, guns loaded and bayonets fixed, moved on the fort, stealthily crossing the soft sand before dawn. Fired on by Southern pickets, they rushed with a cheer across the fort's wet ditch chasing the retreating pickets to the crest of the fort's seaface wall.

From the collection of "Middleton Correspondence 1861-1865," a letter from Susan Middleton to her cousin Harriet tells of a Mr. Gilchrist who blew someone "to atoms" when the Yankees stormed a parapet in the charge. She went on to add, "The gentlemen say this was a shocking waste of powder."

Gilchrist remembered it differently.

"Against the dark sky the dim outline of a human figure could just be discerned. Lt. R.C. Gilchrist, of the Gist Guard, in command of the company, challanged him to know if he was friend or foe. Quick as thought the man's gun was levelled and a ball parted the Lieutenant's hair, the powder blinding his eyes. His 32-pounder, double shotted with grape and cannister, belched forth a reply, the whole load passing through the man's body, cutting him in twain, his discharged rifle dropping in the battery.

"Instantly the whole battery was ablaze. The artillery opened with a murderous hail of grape and cannister, while the musketry poured forth in a steady roll, their balls sent like wind and rain in the face of the foe. As the light of day increased, and the smoke cleared away, the retreating columns of blue coats were seen making for the sand hills."

They took one hundred thirty prisoners and buried one hundred in front of Fort Wagner. A second assault on Wagner on July 18th used forty-two guns and mortars, joined by guns of the fleet. Union losses were heavy, totaling more than 1,500 casualties as men walked shoulder to shoulder across the battlefield to create mass gunfire.

Gilchrist never forgot the aftermath of the fighting, as he recalled:

> "Blood, mud, water, brains and human hair matted together; men lying in every possible attitude, with every conceivable expression on their countenances; their limbs bent into unnatural shapes by the fall of twenty or more feet; the fingers rigid and outstretched, as if they had clutched at the earth to save themselves; pale, beseeching faces, looking out from among the ghastly corpses, with moans and cries for help and water; dying gasps and death struggles.
>
> "All of Sunday was employed in removing the wounded and burying the dead. . . . Wounds being inflicted at such short distance, little could be done save to amputate, and Federal blood flowed by the bucket full."

Gilchrist gave credit to a Union Major who remembered an order from Beauregard.

> "Beauregard directed that special care be taken of the wounded captured at Wagner, as men who were brave enough to go in there deserved the respect of their enemy."

Earlier Beauregard held a council of general officers. It would take 4,000 to drive the Federals off the island. To get that number on the island under cover of darkness in one night with limited transportation was impossible. Gilchrist wrote, "Unwillingly the idea was abandoned. That opportunity was lost." From then on they realized victory was impossible, and their efforts became a holding action and delay.

Yankee seige operations were begun after their second defeat. Union General Gilmore stopped attempting a frontal assault and during the night, through a series of 'parallels,' trenches that ran parallel to Fort Wagner, he was able to move his men forward in stages. Even before the final assault which would give him the prize of Morris

Island, Gilmore ordered Confederate troops to withdraw
from Morris Island and Fort Sumter, or the bombardment
of Charleston would begin. Beauregard called it an act of
inexcusable barbarity for attacking a city of civilians.

'The Swamp Angel,' an affectionate title Union soldiers gave to the gun which could loft 150-pound projectiles
into the city of Charleston, shattered the quiet of the early
hours on August 22, 1863. The heavy gun had been posi-
tioned on a floating mud battery in the marsh of Morris
Island. Before the gun burst on its thirty-sixth round, it had
shaken the city's confidence and caused panic, but the city
failed to surrender.

Gilchrist's family had left Charleston to avoid enemy
shells, leaving the treasured family clock with the Wittpens,
a German family who lived on King Street. A fire in an out
building traveled to the room where the clock had been
safely kept throughout the war. Mrs. Wittpen carried the
clock out of the burning room into her garden and hid it
under a gardenia bush, saving it once again.

For the men at Fort Wagner it became ". . . a period of
simple endurance on Morris Island. Night and day, with
scarcely any intermission, the hurling shell burst over and
within it. Each day, often from early dawn, the New Ironsides or the six monitors, sometimes all together, steamed
up and delivered their terrific broadsides, shaking the fort
to its centre. . . ."

Gilchrist recalled:

"The burning sun of a Southern summer, its heat
intensified by the reflection of the white sand,
scorched and blistered the unprotected garrison, or
the more welcome rain and storm wet them to the
skin. An intolerable stench from the unearthed dead
of the previous conflict, the carcasses of cavalry horses
lying where they fell in the rear, and barrels of putrid
meat thrown out on the beach, sickened the defenders.
. . . Water was scarcer than whiskey. . . . The unventi-
lated bomb-proofs, filled with smoke of lamps and
smell of blood were intolerable, so that one endured

the risk of shot and shell rather then seek its shelter.

". . . each day added to the list of killed and wounded. Amputated limbs were brought out from the hospital and buried in the sand. Often bodies followed them. Only as a special favor, or where high rank claimed the privilege, were the dead carried to the city for interment."

For two months the Confederate force, which never exceeded sixteen hundred men at one time, withstood a better equipped army of over eleven thousand troops, Ironsides, eight monitors and five gunboats. But the long and stubborn defense of Fort Wagner served its purpose.

Gilchrist proudly wrote in a footnote to his later account that, "At West Point there are only two models of fortifications used for purposes of instruction to the Cadets in the art of attack and defense; one of these is Fort Wagner, the other Sebastopol."

In addition to the symbolism of capturing Charleston, it also meant it would be a fairly simple matter to march the few miles to Branchville, seize the railroad there, and aid in splitting Confederate forces. By the 5th of September, General Gilmore was ready to move again.

Shells poured down on the defiant defenders. Gilchrist wrote, "For forty-two consecutive hours this iron hail descended. . . . At one time as many as four shells could be seen at once en route for Wagner. . . . The casualties on that day were one in nine."

Beauregard sent someone to determine the capability of continuing the Fort's defense and the order was given for its evacuation. With the enemy close by, it took place by boat around nine o'clock in the evening. "The soft sand echoed no foot-steps, and no voice was raised above a whisper." By the early hours of September 7, 1863, the garrison had been evacuated safely. Without opposition, Union forces walked into the abandoned fort at daylight.

For Union's General Gilmore, the object of gaining Morris Island was to wipe out resistance on Sumter so the navy's ironclads could move into Charleston Harbor. What

resulted from the stubborn delay caused by the Confederates was the strengthening of batteries on James and
Sullivan Islands, and a new line of inner defenses around
the city. For another eighteen months the Yankee fleet
would remain in the outer harbor viewing the church spires
of Charleston.

CHAPTER FIVE

That Agony is Over

Day after day people gathered in Charleston in 1864 to read the death rolls and hear the whispers that North Carolina was talking terms of peace. Lee had retreated from Gettysburg with heavy losses the year before and many felt, as did Mary Chesnut, that all hope was gone. In 1864, a Confederate dollar was worth seven cents and Mrs. Chesnut paid twenty-four dollars for six spools of thread and thirty-two dollars for "five, miserable, shabby little pocket handkerchiefs."

That year Lincoln was up for re-election. Even with the largest army the world had ever seen, his Union generals lacked significant military victories, and Lincoln's re-election was uncertain. Opposition to the war increased. The year before immigrant mobs in New York City had hunted down blacks, and beaten and lynched them to protest federal conscription. It took five Union Army regiments ordered back from Gettysburg to suppress the rioting mob.

On March 8, 1864, Lincoln appointed Ulysses S. Grant as head of all Union Armies. Grant had won in the west at Fort Donaldson, Vicksburg and Chattanooga, and was now rewarded with the command of 533,000 men. But the long seige at Petersburg tied Grant down, and Sherman was stymied outside Atlanta. The year dragged on with battle-field amputations and military stalemates.

To make matters worse, George McClellan, who had

hesitated as a cautious Union commander and at times defied his President, was nominated as the Democratic party candidate to run against him. The South rejoiced at McClellan's nomination.

In June 1864, the Confederate Congress enacted legislation extending conscription from age seventeen to fifty. Gilchrist was detached from his command to serve as Judge Advocate General in the Departments of South Carolina, Georgia, and Florida and promoted to Captain. As law advisor of that department he authored *General Orders from the Adjutant and Inspector-General's Office of the Confederate States of America* and *The Duties of a Judge Advocate in a Trial Before a General Court Martial*.

This last was to aid officers in the field. Desertions were increasing as men weary of war saw no hope of victory. President Jefferson Davis was struggling to keep the Confederacy alive and decided to replace General Joseph Johnston at Atlanta. Johnston was one of his best commanders, but like Beauregard, not popular with the confederate president. Gilchrist served under both Beauregard and Johnston before war's end.

At Atlanta, the Union's William Tecumseh Sherman sealed off supplies to the railroad hub of the South and shelled the city. After a long standoff Atlanta was finally taken at the end of the summer. Mrs. Chesnut wrote, "Atlanta is gone. That agony is over." Where fighting had been sporadic before and men like Gilchrist had found time to see their families, in 1864 the war went on without letup.

With the Union's superior numbers, a blockade that was choking the South and no foreign intervention on their behalf, their cause seemed doomed. Lincoln was re-elected and the South fought on.

Early in 1865 the defense of Charleston and its emotional symbolism of defiance was outweighed by the need to have trained and disciplined troops to keep Union forces from joining in Virginia. On February 18, 1865, city fathers sent a rowboat out to inform the Yankee fleet that Confederate forces had evacuated Charleston.

Ten days later Gilchrist was promoted to Artillery Major. Accompanying General Hardee into North Carolina, Gilchrist burned the bridge at Cheraw over the Great Peedee River, "with my own hands after all our army had passed over, and the man who assisted me there was shot by my side, his blood spurting over my coat." He fought at Averysboro and Bentonville in North Carolina ". . . and at the last assisted in bearing from the field the last man killed in the war—General Hardee's son."

Richmond, the capital of the Confederacy, surrendered on April 3, 1865. Six days later, Lee surrendered at Appomattox. Skirmishes continued and Gilchrist was in a hand-to-hand fight in Fayetteville with some of Kilpatrick's cavalry and came near to being captured.

The last Confederate commander in the field, Joseph E. Johnston, surrendered April 26, 1865. Gilchrist's military service ended when General Johnston appointed him to be one of the Commissioners of parole. As such he signed, with the Yankee officer, the paroles of the remaining Confederate army. Rebels put down their arms and went home.

Just as the marshes, sand, and pluff mud had hindered Union forces in capturing Morris Island, so the low country's geography protected Charleston from Sherman's marching into the city. Instead his troops marched inland to the state capital at Columbia and Gilchrist's city was saved.

The Civil War brought defeat and poverty to once proud Charleston. Yet poverty created a windfall of misfortune that preserved the magnificent homes which had escaped the great fire of 1861 and the enemy's shelling. There was little money to build anew. Transportation was destroyed, railroads and bridges burned and ruined, and Confederate money and securities were virtually worthless.

In the North, Gilchrist's uncle, Robert Gilchrist of The Glen, was profitably selling land. On June 2, 1865, his uncle conveyed 1,345 Adirondack acres to the Albany firm of Friend Humphrey and Sons for $13,455, half of which went to his sister, Gilchrist's mother. Five hundred dollars at war's end would have a purchasing power of over six thousand dollars today.

In addition, Mary Gilchrist received almost four thousand dollars on March 2, 1866. A legal paper had been drawn up with her brothers on the eve of war indicating a balance due on $10,539 would be paid by 1870. Instead she received it at war's end. The same document had given her brother, Robert Gilchrist, the right to "take and receive rents and profits and make repairs and pay all taxes and other necessary expenses" on the inherited Adirondack lands. Smaller sales gave his sister Mary other money.

Lincoln had been assassinated in April 1865 and Tennessee's Andrew Johnson, who'd been put on the 1864 ticket to recognize those Union men who existed in the South, assumed the presidency and the problems of reconstruction. Eleven seceded states had to be brought back into the Union.

Tennessee was readmitted in 1866, and the following year the Reconstruction Act divided the remaining ten Confederate states into five military districts, each governed by a Union general. Andrew Johnson, at odds with Congress when he tried to implement Lincoln's plan, was impeached but not convicted, and remained in office until the next election put Grant in the White House.

In the summer of 1866, Gussie and Robert traveled from Charleston to New York to visit his Uncle Robert in the northern mountains. Steamer lines had started up again after the war and Robert booked passage for them to New York City. From there they could take the night boat up the Hudson to Albany, and then the train to Saratoga.

Stagecoaches ran regularly from Saratoga to points north. Leaving the heat of Charleston, it would be Gussie's first visit to the cool northern mountains and a needed change. Their second daughter, eleven-month-old Mary, had died that June from what the death certificate listed as the effects of teething.

The great northern wilderness was now called the Adirondacks. A comparison would be striking—the flatness of their beloved Charleston, so close to the water level of the harbor, with the wild beauty of the mountain scenery. Unlike the South, there was no devastation from war for battlegrounds never extended farther north than Pennsylvania.

Uncle Robert's home at The Glen, a hamlet in the Town of Johnsburg, sat close to the Hudson River and what was the main road north to Wevertown, although roads in the Adirondacks were not paved until well into the next century. It was a comfortable home, much bigger than the others at The Glen, with barns and out buildings. There were two cows, twenty-five sheep, a horse named Prince and a mare named after Robert and Gussie's little Emma. After the confinements of war-torn Charleston, four-year-old Emma happily played outside in the grass with her dolls while her parents enjoyed Uncle Robert's hospitality.

The house was comfortably furnished with carpets, sofas, rocking chairs, wash stands, mattresses of straw and moss, looking glasses, clocks, and sixty books. Various wines, bottles of champagne and bourbon whiskey were stocked in the house as well, for Mary Gilchrist's brother apparently held more liberal views about such vices.

Over a glass of sherry in the evening, the nephew and uncle could discuss the new Adirondack railway that was being brought north from Saratoga. Not only had Uncle Robert been a backer of the Warrensburg Railroad, but many of his securities were in such railroad bonds as Illinois Central, Erie, Union Pacific, and the Harlem Railroad. The post-war growth of rail transportation was becoming a national conversation.

After putting Emma to bed, Gussie could join their talks, telling her husband's uncle about her Charleston cousin, James Shoolbred Gibbes, an early stockholder in the South Carolina Railroad Company. Railroads would be as much of their conversations that summer at The Glen as stories of the war and affairs in the South.

Back in Charleston, Gussie's mother, Anne Roper Gibbes, was writing to her daughter of household news and the city's summer fevers:

Courtesy of Mary Anne Cunningham

Gilchrist's uncle, another Robert Gilchrist, built this home at The Glen in the Adirondacks. It later became the Grove Hotel.

Courtesy of the Gibbes Museum of Art

Emma S. Gilchrist as a child. Miniature watercolor on ivory, artist unknown.

". . . I have entirely recovered from the effects of my last attack of chills and fever. Adé is also quite well I am thankful to say, but Mrs. G. has not been very well, however she desires her love to Robert and yourself, and bids me say she feels much better. . . . The city is not very healthy just at this time, the broken bone fever has been prevailing very generally, at first it was mild, and people joked each other about being in the fashion, but it is no longer a joke, if taken in hand without loss of time it yields readily to medicine, but otherwise it takes congestive and typhoid forms, it has been fatal to several young people. . . .

"I saw Dr. Mitchell this morning, he mentioned that he had a sleepless and anxious night; on yesterday four of his family were in bed with this fever, and last night little Legere was desperately ill, he thinks him out of danger today; on parting the Dr. said 'what hard times Mrs. Gibbes.'

"I have enclosed some extracts for Robert's perusal of the doings of our August Legislature, the principles of the chivalrous South have really improved on the example set them by the Northern Congress. The Apostle says truly 'evil communications corrupt good manners.' Has not the Serpent left a long trail? Adé desires her love to Emma—says she is looking for an answer to her letter. How we do long for those little pattering feet. . . . All here desire much love to Robert, Emma and yourself in which united,

your mother."

They returned to Charleston in September, and shortly thereafter Robert's mother drew up her will, dividing her estate between Robert and his sister Mary Elizabeth. Gussie was included as a survivor of any inheritance, but ". . . as to the moiety hereby bequeathed and given to my daughter the said Mrs. Mary Elizabeth Baker it is likewise my intention and my will further is that the same is Hers absolutely not subject to the contracts, engagements, debts or penalties of her present or any future husband."

Mary Elizabeth had married the Reverend Archibald

Baker of Fernandina, Florida, a widower with four children. There is no evidence that Mary Gilchrist disliked her daughter's husband, and her mother may have simply wanted to protect her daughter's inheritance.

Uncle Robert also made his will in 1866, naming his Charleston nephew as executor rather than his only son. Robert's Adirondack cousin, Ambrose Spencer Gilchrist, had enlisted during the war in Company E, 63rd Regiment at Albany, but never seemed to win his father's approval.

The following year on August 19, 1867, at the age of seventy, Robert's mother, Mary Gilchrist died. With what he inherited from his mother, and probably encouraged by his uncle, he decided to build a home in the Adirondacks. And like John Thurman who first bought the land Robert inherited, Robert Cogdell Gilchrist began to think of how it could be commercially developed.

CHAPTER SIX

The Inheritance

When Mary Gilchrist married her Charleston first cousin, Robert Budd Gilchrist, she brought to the marriage thousands of acres of land in the Adirondacks that would one day belong to her son, Robert Cogdell Gilchrist. Her mother, Elizabeth Roosevelt Gilchrist, had inherited land from the divided estate of her uncle, John Thurman.

Thurman was born in New York City in 1730. His sister, Elizabeth Thurman, married Nicholas Roosevelt III (1715-1769). It was their daughter, Elizabeth Roosevelt, who married Robert August Gilchrist, the third son of the Scottish immigrant, Adam Gilchrist.

Thurman died in 1809. One half of the wilderness tract went to a nephew, Ralph Thurman, who had acted as a land agent for his Uncle. The other half was equally divided between Mary's mother, Elizabeth Roosevelt Gilchrist, and her brother, Nicholas Roosevelt IV (1760-1838).

When Mary Gilchrist's parents died, she and her two brothers, Robert and John, inherited the Thurman lands. Leasing, selling, and buying other land continued for years. The number of family-owned acres fluctuated from time to time, but was always substantial.

Thurman became a successful New York merchant although he said when he first commenced business, "Times were dull and trade light."

He put up a notice that his store would be open only

two days a week, and proceeded to do more business in those two days than before. The rest of the week he worked for whatever wages and employment he could find and his circumstances improved. Thurman enjoyed telling the young men he employed about the early struggles he faced and particularly about the one incident which changed the direction of his life.

As his trade increased and times got better he bought a horse and shay and spent some time riding around the city. "On a certain day he passed a man in the street to whom he owed a sum of money. The man stopped and took a long gaze after the horse, carriage and driver. Thurman construed the man's thoughts . . . 'Young man, you had better pay your debts before you drive about in such style.'" He drove home at once, sold his horse and carriage, and paid the man his money, believing that man's gaze caused him to reflect and changed the course of his life.

A general importer of dry goods, his firm was located on Wall Streeet at the corner of South. The firm also maintained and owned a marine slip or dock on the East River. His accounts revealed that he carried on an extensive importing and exporting business with firms in London, Belfast, and in France and the West Indies.

In 1765, Thurman was active in the 'Sons of Liberty' who opposed the Stamp Act that placed taxes on legal documents and papers of all kinds. By 1769, he was a member of New York's Chamber of Commerce and the following year appointed by the Colonial Legislature to be a commissioner, along with Patrick Henry and other Virginians, to plan trade with the Indians.

While he had sympathized earlier with those who resisted the taxes the British were asking the colonies to pay, he refused to support the break with England. Seen as a charming man, apparently his personality and the friends and connections he made enabled him to remain neutral during the war. After independence he was elected as assemblyman to the new State Legislature.

The state of New York was impoverished after the

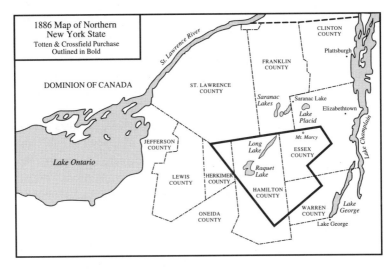

Map showing the Totten & Crossfield purchase from which John Thurman bought some 50,000 acres.

National Portrait Gallery

Engraving of John Thurman (Doctor Hill), whose home was on Elm Hill, in the town of Johnsburg.

Revolutionary War and eager to sell land. Governor George Clinton recognized claims to certain townships in the Totten and Crossfield Purchase that had been negotiated with the Indians before the war. The large tract was divided into townships, and John Thurman paid 1,400 pounds sterling for Township Number 12's patent of 25,200 acres. A year later he added an additional 23,920 acres with the acquisition of Township Number 13.

Roger G. Kennedy writes in his book, *Orders from France*, "We have only a few scraps of paper to tell us anything about this wonderful man, who tried to create an industrial complex amid the granite outcrops, bogs, boulders, and blue mountains of the Adirondacks, where the Hudson is a roistering, unpredictable young river."

Thurman's lands were boulder riddled, but he encouraged settlement and built a community, reportedly meeting immigrant boats and describing land and opportunity to the new arrivals. His first home was built at Elm Hill Farm, two miles south of today's hamlet of Johnsburg in upstate New York. "It was a frontier citadel so important that for many years the territory west of the Hudson River and north of Athol was known among the friends in England, Ireland and America as Elm Hill."

With the help of young men he brought up from New York City, he built a dam on Beaver Creek, today's Mill Creek, and erected a sawmill and a grist mill. While he was attending to his New York business, he gave specific instructions for the welfare of his northern community. In a letter to William Cameron he wrote: "It is difficult to instruct in such a variety of business as there is to be done at the Hill. Frugality and care must extend to every transaction, as to provision for man and beast, the best store will soon be gone if not prudently used. Meat once a day is enough for health and by browsing the cattle much may be saved and the cattle better kept."

He made suggestions as to what crops should be planted and where. "Summer wheat on the moist ground south of the house. . . . It will be well to open the ditch at

Photograph by Wes Pelkey

Elizabeth Roosevelt Gilchrist, maternal grandmother of
Robert Cogdell Gilchrist, is buried in the family plot in
Wevertown, New York. John Thurman is also buried here.

the Beaver dam to let the water off as early in the spring as
you can, a day or twos work I think will do this business. . . .
As to the goods on hand they are meant for the improvement of the Hill and to assist the settlers and are to be used
as so much cash paid for labour as you may want it."

While Thurman gave advice to Mr. Cameron on man-
aging the settlement's business affairs, he also offered
encouragement, "I know it will require great attention in
you but don't be discouraged. Do your business with firm-
ness, make all your bargains fair and clear and should the
bargains so made turn out bad, fulfill them with honor, but
don't let it discourage you. . . ."

Eventually he had a store and a distillery built; a mill
for making potash; a woolen factory later changed to a cotton factory; and reportedly the first calico printing mill in
America in 1797.

One journal described him at sixty-one as ". . . an
amiable man, who besides being well-informed, possessed a
gayety quite rare for a man somewhat advanced in years."

He lived for another twenty years, until gored by his own enraged bull he was trying to control. A quote from the family journal in Charleston records the way he died and adds, ". . . he probably imagined he had mastered all knowledge, even how to make a successful crop out of stony ground."

Thurman lies buried in a small cemetery in Wevertown in a plot surrounded by a low cut-stone wall. Within the family area are headstones for Thurman and his niece, Elizabeth Roosevelt, and her husband, Robert August Gilchrist, the maternal grandparents of the Confederate officer from Charleston. The dream of creating a commercial empire in the northern wilderness died with him, for although a successful tannery was built in Wevertown in the 1830's, without Thurman's energetic presence, the area saw little further growth.

Because of the death of his nephew, Ralph Thurman, the executor of Thurman's will, it wasn't until August 25, 1843, that the large Thurman holdings were settled. It was Mary Gilchrist's brother, Robert, a lawyer and businessman, who petitioned to administer the estate.

Born in New York City in 1795, this Robert Gilchrist was educated at Columbia College, and began business as a merchant in the city of Albany around 1820. On December 16, 1823 he married the daughter of State Chief Justice Ambrose Spencer. A newspaper described her as "a lady of remarkable beauty and intelligence." Laura Spencer Gilchrist died in 1825 leaving an infant son, Ambrose Spencer Gilchrist. Her husband never remarried, and after her death he moved to New York City and established an importing business there, much as Thurman had done.

Unlike Judge Robert Budd Gilchrist, Mary's husband, her brother Robert never used a middle name on any of the numerous legal papers and deeds bearing his name. He is most easily identified as Uncle Robert to Mary's children, and especially close to his Charleston nephew. In the 1840's, he retired to The Glen, his home in the Adirondacks.

The Glen lies along the Hudson River in the southeast

Courtesy of Lewis Waddell

Covered bridge at The Glen, built in 1816, crossed the Hudson River connecting the towns of Johnsburg, Chester, Thurman and Warrensburg.

corner of the 130,000 acres that make up today's town of Johnsburg. In 1865, Uncle Robert was one of seven families living at The Glen. The state census of agricultural statistics that year shows him owning 100 acres of improved acreage and 3,000 unimproved acres. At that time the value of his farm at The Glen was valued at $5,000, a considerable sum for that period.

Described as being ". . . of almost unbounded business capacity," he was an early backer in the 1830's of the never-built Warren County Railroad and had a tannery built at The Glen, leasing it to others to run. The mountain tanneries brought employment and settlers, and provided the leather for shoes, saddles, harnesses, and everyday goods.

A covered bridge built in 1816 crossed the Hudson River at The Glen and formed the junction of four towns—Warrensburg, Chester, Thurman and Johnsburg. There was no depot at The Glen until years after the Adirondack track was laid from Saratoga to North Creek. However, trains stopped at The Glen to let off freight and passengers.

When he decided to travel north with his wife and young daughter only a year after Appomattox, Robert Cogdell Gilchrist could have arrived by either rail or stagecoach.

A letter to his wife from her mother in Charleston, dated September 20, 1866, read, "My dear Gussie, Nearly a week has elapsed since I have had the pleasure of receiving any intelligence of your party but I have comforted myself with a number of pleasant conjectures, among them is the agreeable one, that you are gone on a pleasant excursion."

In a postscript she adds, "I have this minute received yrs. 14th and rejoice to learn you are all well, and with faces set homeward, will be still more delighted to see the owners of the dear faces. Mrs. Gilchrist begs that Robert will bring you all by land, as Mr. John Gilchrist says the expense is only $4.60 more than a sea voyage." While Mary's son was staying with Uncle Robert at The Glen, her other brother, John Thurman Gilchrist, was visiting in Charleston.

It took days to travel between Charleston and upstate New York and the journey was carried on by steamer, stagecoach, or where available, by rail. During the war, Congress had chartered the construction of the Union Pacific Railroad, the first of the transcontinental systems. It was subsidized by the federal government with bonuses and land grants. Dr. Thomas Durant, its vice-president and the man overseeing its building, also became interested in a line for the Adirondacks.

By 1863, Durant and some New York City investors sought to build a line between Saratoga and North Creek. Over 700,000 acres were given to the newly organized Adirondack Company for the proposed route; construction began in 1864. As the prime mover in the construction of the Union Pacific transcontinental railroad, it is likely Durant invested his money from that into the Adirondack Company's railway.

Had John Thurman been alive, he would have welcomed the iron horse and the commercial growth it could bring to northern towns on its route. Uncle Robert, with his earlier interest in the railroads, understood the possibilities for development of the lands owned by the Gilchrists, and surely pointed out such possibilities to his nephew.

The wonder of being alive after what he had seen of war—remembering the moment when the enemy's gunpowder blinded him as the shot parted his hair, friends killed in midsentence—these and other painful memories must have surfaced for Gilchrist as he journeyed to the Adirondacks. Always a Unionist in his beliefs, inventive and creative in his thinking, he was a leader of men and anxious to seek a future in the North where the family lands and opportunity waited. His heritage, his Charleston years, wartime action—all affected who he was—and who he would become.

CHAPTER SEVEN

In the Mountains

With the South in disarray, it is easy to imagine that Gilchrist believed his future lay in the North. In 1866, one year after the war ended, and the summer that Gussie and Robert visited at The Glen, people in the North returned to everyday business and New York state bought seven hundred acres of forest in Clinton County to supply wood for the prison system. From that time to the present, the state has been buying up Adirondack acres in an effort to protect its natural resources.

Those resources consist of almost three thousand lakes and ponds, and more than 1,500 miles of rivers which are fed by 30,000 miles of brooks and streams.

Adirondack country's northern border is almost to Canada, with Vermont and Lake Champlain on the east. New York City lies some two hundred miles to the south, while the foothills begin about fifty miles north of the state capital at Albany. Utica is the major westernmost city lying just beyond the blue line of today's Adirondack Park.

In 1866, nineteen-year-old Verplanck Colvin began mapping the Adirondacks. Even before Colvin surveyed and lobbied to protect all he saw, interest in exploring the area came from a Williams College professor, Ebenezer Emmons, who led a group to the high peaks in the 1830's. He was the first to climb and name the highest peak Mt. Marcy, after a New York governor. But other than the early interest of John Thurman and a few land speculators, and the unsuccessful attempt to colonize a few utopian communities, new settlers instead trekked to recently opened fertile lands in the west. Farming had never been easy in the northern mountains of New York what with the rocky soil, harsh winters and short growing season.

The year 1816 was called the "Year Without Summer." Buds and fruit were frozen in May; ice formed half an inch thick and corn was killed; frost and ice were common, killing almost every green thing even in July. Men picked up odd jobs to supplement family income, and still do. Farming is not what one associates with the Adirondacks.

A letter in 1867 from Uncle Robert to his Charleston nephew calls forth a bucolic scene at The Glen. ". . . my two cows filled six tin pans (you saw the pans) last nights milking—and the woman has made 12 pounds of fine yellow butter the past week and the churn now full to beat out."

In June, he wrote of the "difficulty in seeing the passerby on the road side through the foliage and flowers now on the circle before my windows. I cut the grass from the lawn that feeds my horses—you would want a Charleston Detective to hunt up Emma if she was now on it with the Dolls."

Images of forested mountains, deep blue lakes, and a rugged life in the outdoors are more often associated with the Adirondacks. During the last glacial period the mountains were covered by an ice sheet. The retreating glaciers rounded off mountain tops and created spectacular gorges, waterfalls, and thousands of lakes and ponds. Five ranges of ancient mountains run from northeast to southwest, nearly parallel, with axes about eight miles apart, a part of the precambrian rock of Canada. Verplanck Colvin eventually surveyed it all.

What Gilchrist saw in 1866 was a land untouched by war's destruction. He was the Southerner travelling north while others hurried to the south, hastily throwing a few things into a case made of carpet material and earning them the ignominius label of 'carpetbaggers.'

Another who travelled a shorter distance to the north

at the same time as Gilchrist was William Murray, a minister from Connecticut. He had visited the northern mountains in 1864 and written about them for a Connecticut newspaper. By 1868 he had been invited to minister to the fashionable pastorate of a Boston Congregational Church, and while there he continued to write Adirondack sketches that eventually were published in 1869 as *Adventures in the Wilderness* or *Camp Life in the Adirondacks.*

A remarkable reaction to the book followed, and the history books credit Murray with a 'rush to the Adirondacks.' In addition to writing about his adventures in the mountains, 'Adirondack Murray' as he would always be called, had produced a guidebook giving routes, hotels, what to do, and what to wear in the Adirondack wilderness. Perhaps because he was a clergyman his words were taken as gospel, and the stampede was on.

Although the book created a great interest in the mountains that would have far-reaching consequences, many were disappointed with reality, for the hotels were, at first, few and primitive. That would change.

Keeping in mind that the Civil War only interrupted the market revolution which began with the advent of railroads, Murrays' book came at a time when the mountains were accessible through a series of trains, steamships and stagecoaches. The country was ready to move forward in most any kind of development. The businessman would come to be the hero; legislatures were supportive of industrial growth, and the public enthusiastic about seeing for itself the wonders of a trip to Murray's mountains.

Meshing nicely with the public's interest in seeing the attractions Murray praised, were the newly built lodges or hotels soon available in a variety of price ranges. Resorts well known today like Lake George, Schroon Lake and Lake Placid came into being. Parasoled ladies in rustling long skirts and high button shoes, along with their dapper escorts, strolled on green lawns. The city sport searched for a local guide to take him fishing and hunting. Tourism was to become the industry which supported many who lived there, and is still the major income for the area today.

The two-year college in northern New York known as Paul Smith's, with majors in hotel business and forestry, has historic ties to a colorful mountain host from that period. Paul Smith built a hotel northwest of Saranac Lake on Lake St. Regis, and throughout the end of the nineteenth century attracted society figures from New York City.

Perhaps the most famous of Paul Smith's guests was a very sick man. Dr. Edward Livingston Trudeau arrived in poor health, expecting to die; instead he recovered, and went on to become a pioneer in the treatment of tuberculosis. The healing air that Reverend Murray wrote about brought other invalids north as well. Trudeau stayed and opened his Adirondack Cottage Sanitorium, offering those individuals hope.

Many believed the curative qualities of the mountain air came from the healthy forest. The idea grew that the cool, clean air of the Adirondack forest promoted stronger bodies to resist tuberculosis, or what was then called consumption. The village of Saranac Lake grew into a cottage industry of homes that took in the ailing and the second story 'cure porch,' where sleeping in the outdoor air was supposed to help treat the disease, can still be seen.

Paul Smith, flamboyant host and serious businessman, was not only responsible for bringing Dr. Trudeau to the Adirondacks, but also people like the Vanderbilts and the Harrimans. To some he sold land, beginning the era of the Great Camps built by the Gilded Age millionaires.

Most of the buildings on their large estates were made of lumber. The mountains held a variety of trees, depending on the elevation—maples, birches, balsam and tamarack, ash and poplar, as well as the ubiquitous pine and spruce. Once covered with tall white pines that shipbuilders coveted for their masts, the forests were badly harvested, as if holding an inexhaustible supply.

Gilchrist shared that view of his Adirondack lands and wrote, "Immediately at hand is a boundless supply of the finest hardwood such as black ash, maple, butternut, etc., as well as the other woods used in the manufacture of furniture. The country around also supplies more wood than a factory could consume, and the day is not far distant when the hum of the spindle and the busy clank of machinery will wake the echoes of these mountains."

Vast tracts of the Adirondacks were sold to the timber industry. Lumbering drives occurred as early as 1813 and grew in number throughout the century. Logs could be floated down the rivers into the rushing water of springtime, enabling the timber men to go deeper into the woods and use oxen and horses to drag loaded sleds over frozen roads. With the spring thaw, the smallest stream could move logs. It was dangerous work that could kill men or take out bridges.

The mountains were being stripped first for lumber, but also for the hemlock bark used in the tanneries where animal hides were made into leather. By 1840 there were 270 tanneries in the Adirondacks producing various grades of leather, creating an important industry in the 19th century. Those who lumbered in the woods, stripping the bark from trees and leaving the logs to rot, wiped out the once abundant supply of Adirondack hemlock.

But the threat to the healing Adirondack forests came from another source when the paper making industry discovered spruce was its best wood. More paper mills were built and New York state came to lead in the production of paper. Not everyone saw this as a positive good. Some worried about the destruction of the watershed forests.

The call for state protection of the forest came even before the Civil War when an Albany journalist, Samuel H. Hammond wrote in his book, *Wild Northern Scenes*, "Had I my way, I would mark out a circle of a hundred miles in diameter and throw around it the protecting aegis of the constitution. I would make it a forest forever." Another writer, Charles Loring Brace, praising the magnificent mountains, declared them fit "to make a Central Park for the world," and tied the word Park to the Adirondacks.

Yellowstone had been established as a park by an act of

Congress in 1872. In 1883, New York State withdrew its remaining Adirondack lands for sale and appropriated money to purchase additional Adirondack forestland. Two years later the Governor signed a law establishing a forest preserve. It was the men of power and wealth in New York City, worried about the city's water supply and the relationship of the watershed provided by the mountain forests, that prompted the state legislature to respond.

Largely through Verplanck Colvin's persistance, legislation was passed in 1892 which established the Adirondack Park. The boundaries were drawn on the state's map as a blue line, identifying the park as 'within the blue line.' Additional acres were added until today's park has an area of six million acres; larger than Yellowstone, our largest national park in the contiguous forty-eight states. It represents twenty percent of New York State.

Unlike Yellowstone, the Adirondack Park is roughly forty percent public and sixty percent privately owned. More than 2,500,000 acres of publicly-owned Forest Preserve are protected as 'forever wild' by the State Constitution. The Adirondack Park Agency (APA) was created in 1971 as the authority to protect the resources of the forest preserve and control the development of the 3.5 million acres held privately.

Being told what owners could do with their land was not accepted easily, and the APA remains controversial even in a time of environmental concerns.

As large, privately owned acreage is sold off, the threat today comes from developers who look at the mountains as a last frontier for second homes for prosperous urban dwellers. Timber companies who previously managed their woodlands as a natural resource have also become interested in land development.

Interest in developing the Adirondacks has been cyclical—from the land grants the newly formed Federal government sold to John Thurman and other land speculators like Aaron Burr and Gouverneur Morris—down to today's condominium developers of second homes.

An artist's sketch of Inglewood Mansion, drawn by Lou Sassi.

Robert Cogdell Gilchrist came to the Adirondacks with the idea of developing land, too. Envisioning a variety of commercial enterprises springing forth on land he owned along the route of the new Adirondack Railway, he built a home on lot 46 in Totten and Crossfield's 12th Township and called it 'Inglewood.'

The locals called it a mansion, for the tall white house set on a hill at the end of a long drive between newly planted maple trees was far grander than other homes in Wevertown. There were four fireplaces, speaking tubes between rooms, a pretty blue and white striped wallpaper picked out by Gussie for an upstairs bedroom, and servants quarters in the rear. Its two deep-seated bay windows provided a magnificent view of the Hudson River below and looked out at Gage Mountain.

Men like Gilchrist who dreamed of the kind of development which would bring progress to their communities, and incidentally wealth to themselves, existed in great numbers after the war. Railroads fed those dreams. The tracks of the Adirondack Company were being built along the Hudson through Gilchrist land. Trains would be bringing tourists and new industries to the mountains. Gilchrist had a dream for the mountains, too.

CHAPTER EIGHT

Railroad Fever

Andrew Jackson, President when Gilchrist was born, was the first American President to ride on a train. During Gilchrist's lifetime, from Jackson to Theodore Roosevelt, it was an era of railroad building and rapid industrial development. America's industrial revolution, like England's, would require fast, heavy duty land transportation that railways can provide.

The South with its many connecting waterways for transportation, did not invest in railroads to the degree the North did. Using rivers and streams as watery highways, an antebellum advertisement in the Charleston *Courier*, said, "Persons wishing to take passage or to send freight down by this boat are informed that she will not stop unless there is a white flag hoisted at the point they wish to get in, or where their freight is to be taken from." The papers listed packet departure times and destinations.

Gussie's cousin, James Shoolbred Gibbes, was a stockholder in the South Carolina Railroad Company. As early as February 1829, when Jackson was about to be sworn in, construction began on a five-foot gauge line from Charleston to Hamburg, South Carolina. This line was the first in the country to begin scheduled passenger cars pulled by a steam locomotive named 'The Best Friend of Charleston.'

Other members of Charleston's commercial community, like Gussie's cousin, sought to tap the trade of the new

Wevertown Hotel in the 1870's.

The Harrington farm was down the road from the Gilchrist mansion.

southwest and compete for the rice, cotton and other goods being shipped out of Mobile and New Orleans. When the entire line to Hamburg was completed in 1833 it ran 136 miles and was then the longest operating line in the country. It eventually became part of the 8,000-mile Southern Railway system.

But as the railway drew near the city, the company was kept from laying tracks to the wharves by the city fathers. Charleston's golden age of commerce lasted as long as the age of sail, and while outwardly still the grand city, its economic decline began with competition from other forms of transportation.

Rails were used by both sides to transport troops and supplies during the war, but the North had an advantage. It had more miles of track, and track that ran to the west. At war's end, a great part of the South's rail system had been destroyed. The war only interrupted the growth of rail systems, and at the close of that conflict, a new era of railroad building began.

The importance of a rail system that would link the agriculture, industry and commerce of the two coasts and open the great plains of the west to settlement resulted in congress passing the Pacific Railroad Act in 1862, providing government loan bonds and land grants.

Dr. Thomas Durant, a graduate of Albany Medical College, had earlier abandoned the practice of medicine and gone into business. At the start of the war he became interested in the transcontinental line, became the company's vice president and was a leading figure in its construction. The Canadian Pacific Railroad was bringing their line from the West and the lines were joined in Utah.

Before its completion, Durant became interested in building a railroad into the Adirondacks to bring out its ore and lumber, and perhaps bring in tourists and other business. Saratoga had earlier been connected to Albany. Durant organized the Adirondack Company under an act of the state legislature acquiring all rights, privileges and franchises of the old Adirondack Estate and Railroad Company.

Courtesy of The Adirondack Museum
Dr. Thomas Durant, builder of the Adirondack Railway.

Courtesy of The Johnsburg Historical Society and Rosine Gardner
"The Gables," home of Dr. Durant at North Creek.

Courtesy of The Adirondack Museum
The first train of the Adirondack Railroad, 1865.

Courtesy of The Adirondack Museum
Photograph of the North Creek Depot by Seneca Ray
Stoddard.

Eventually Durant brought the line from Saratoga to his home in North Creek, New York, and the first train was the captured rebel locomotive 'Major General Hancock.' For a good part of the sixty miles of track, the line follows the Hudson River on its east, from Hadley, through Stony Creek, Thurman, The Glen, Washburn's Eddy, Riverside and on to North Creek.

From The Glen to Riverside, Gilchrist had inherited John Thurman's riverfront land. On June 28, 1870, he signed an agreement with Dr. Durant conveying a total of 1,542 acres for $12,000 down and another $12,000 to be made in two payments of $6,000 each on the same day in 1871 and 1872. Whether Gilchrist believed this would insure Durant granting him a depot on the line is not documented.

With the railroad's completion, a *New York Times* editorial in 1864 predicted the Adirondacks would become a suburb of New York. While the southern end of the track through relatively flat land was put down easily, the steep and winding northern half presented more of a challenge.

The Glens Falls Messenger on July 8, 1864, carried a story from a newspaper in Saratoga. "The work on the Adirondack road, northward from this place, is making commendable progress. The dearth of laborers is seriously felt, but some four hundred are now actively engaged on different portions of the first fourteen miles. Before our people are fairly aware of it, the steam-horse will be making his daily trip into the Northern wilds."

After the railway was completed, that daily trip sometimes ran into difficulties. *The Glens Falls Republican* reported, "Last Tuesday the wind gathered all the spare snow in that locality and piled it into a cut on the Adirondack Railroad between Jessup's Landing and South Corinth so that it took six hours to dig a train through."

Weather wasn't the only problem in bringing the trains into the north country. The same newspaper wrote, "A train on the Adirondack Railroad recently converted a yoke of oxen, three cows and a heifer into fresh beef in the twinkling of an eye, when coming around the corner at The

Glen. The cattle were standing on the track and the engine ran over them."

For all roads reporting earnings in 1851, there were 8,836 miles operated by railroads. By 1871, that had grown to 44,614 miles. By that year the sixty miles of track required by Durant's charter were completed; the Adirondack Company was reporting that passenger travel over the road in 1871 was a third more than the year before; tourists came by the thousands to the region on the trains, and stage-coaches were at the depots and brought tourists to points even further north.

Jim Shaughnessy writes in his book, *Delaware and Hudson*, "Wagner Palace Cars were run directly from New York over the Hudson River Railroad and the D&H to Saratoga, then on the Adirondack to North Creek, arriving there early in the morning. Most of the remainder of the day was spent on the stage coach, jolting over the steep, rough roads to the many resort hotels nestled in the mountains. At the round trip excursion fare of $18.25, thousands of city dwellers made the combined rail-stage-steamboat trip to Raquette Lake and its surroundings each summer. In addition to the hotels, hundreds of summer cottages and children's camps in the mountains developed a passenger trade for the line that lasted eighty-five seasons."

The line ended just above North Creek at the time it ran out of available funds. The panic of 1873 ended any hope of pushing further, but the railroad was responsible for the growth of towns along its route. There were other consequences as well. The locomotives that spewed sparks and hot coals were identified as the leading cause of forest fires, and threatened the value of the woods as a watershed. Eventually laws were passed requiring railroads to use spark arresters on their locomotives.

Traffic was brisk on the Adirondack line. *the Glens Falls Republican* wrote in August 1872, "A subscriber at Riverside on the Adirondack Railroad says: 'The arrivals and departures from this station average over fifty passengers daily. We have the best depot on the road.'" The company had spent six million getting the line into operation.

Gilchrist wanted a depot on the line near his Inglewood home. A bridge crossing the Hudson near this depot could lead to Chester and unite it with the town of Johnsburg, in his own words, "furnishing the inhabitants of Chester with a nearer and easier access to the Adirondack Railway."

Just as the railroads met the need for transportation and communication in the rapidly expanding nation of the nineteenth century, so did the bridges spanning obstructions and opening new routes. Thomas Pope had written as early as 1811, "It is a notorious fact that there is no country of the world which is more in need of good and permanent bridges than the United States of America." In his "A Treatise on Bridge Architecture, in Which the Superior Advantages of the Flying Pendant Lever Bridge Are Fully Proved," he said, "Let the broad arc the spacious Hudson stride."

A bridge is a work of art, and Gilchrist was an artist. He could envision a bridge striding the Hudson River near his home where the river is neither wide nor deep. If a bridge was built near Washburn's Eddy where a depot was to be granted by Durant, passengers getting off could cross the bridge to Chestertown.

In Gilchrist's words, "the trade and travel of the whole country around will naturally radiate. The distance to Chestertown is shortened by two miles, and the steep and dangerous mountain roads are avoided. The depot will be but four miles from Weavertown [sic], by a road of easy grade, and about the same distance from the western settlements of Johnsburg."

Gilchrist was a well-read man who followed current events. One of the big events of that time was the Roebling Bridge begun in 1869 which crossed the East River and joined Brooklyn with Manhattan. Newspapers covered the suspension bridge's progress.

Gilchrist had much in common with Washington Roebling, the bridge's builder. Roebling had enlisted in the Union Army in 1861, the year Gilchrist and Gussie married.

Courtesy of Richard S. Allen

Advertisement from a *Directory of American Bridge Building Companies 1840-1900*.

From the R.P.I. Yearbook, *Transit 1897*

Charles MacDonald, bridge engineer for Gilchrist's bridge.

Like Gilchrist, he saw action in battles, rose to be an officer, and letters home told nothing of the dangers he faced. By coincidence, it was Washington Roebling's second wife, Cornelia Witsell Farrow of Charleston, who restored the William Gibbes house on South Battery many years later.

Both men were quiet and introspective, small in physical stature, and had some sympathy for the other side and the terrible loss of life. Both shared the most influential experience of men of that generation—the Civil War.

Each man was acquainted with Charles MacDonald. MacDonald had graduated from Rennselaer Polytechnic Institute at Troy, New York as a civil engineer, where Roebling also graduated. He had been in charge of surveys and construction of the Pennsylvania and Reading railroad, and in 1868 moved to New York City and opened an office at 80 Broadway. He was also appointed a board trustee representing the City of New York during the construction of the bridge going up over the East River, forever known as the Brooklyn Bridge.

It is not clear when or how the engineer MacDonald and the Charleston attorney Gilchrist first met. The engineer was listed in the New York City directory in 1870 as "Burton and MacDonald, Engineers and Contractors for the construction of iron and wooden bridges." Perhaps Gilchrist chose him from the directory. MacDonald became a highly respected bridge builder, taught at and became a trustee of R.P.I., and in a tribute from his fellow engineers was elected to the presidency of the American Society of Civil Engineers in 1908.

His plans for the Hawkesbury Bridge in Australia were chosen by a board of British engineers in 1887 after competition with British, French, and German engineers and involved the deepest foundations attempted up to that time. He is listed in *American Men of Science* and *Who Was Who in America*. It would seem that Gilchrist had chosen a man to build his Adirondack bridge who knew how to build bridges that would last.

In the 1870's contractors for bridges bought wire rope

from the Roebling's & Sons Company in Trenton, New Jersey, and had it shipped to a building site. A crew would come from Trenton to string the long cables across. There were other small competing businesses, but given Roebling's reputation by the end of the Civil War, it is unlikely that wire was sought from any other source. In addition, the bridge's engineer, Charles MacDonald, had graduated with Washington Roebling in the small class of 1847 at R.P.I.

Railroads caused the transition to iron bridges from wooden because of the weight of the 'iron horse,' but Gilchrist's bridge was not to be for railroads. It was, however, to be an iron bridge, the first suspension bridge across the Hudson River—fifty years before the building of the Bear Mountain Bridge and sixty years before the George Washington Bridge was completed.

What the local businessmen who had always lived in the area thought when plans for the Southerner's bridge were announced and work begun, can only be imagined. Thirty-four local men had died fighting the Confederacy, and returned amputees were living in the area. Reconciling his mother's north and his father's south after the Civil War became a lifetime challenge, and while his move north and his bridge was a symbol of reaching out to the other side, not everyone was of a like mind.

CHAPTER NINE

Let the Broad Arc Begin

No permit was needed when Gilchrist decided to span the Hudson River with a suspension bridge. There were no federal or state inspectors or regulators at that time—no inland waterway agency overseeing travel or building on the river north of Troy. The Interstate Commerce Commission was not established until 1887 and not until 1940 did it cover domestic water carriers. At his own expense, Gilchrist was free to place a bridge between land he owned on either side of the Hudson.

A suspension bridge has certain advantages over other bridges in that it needs no center support and can be put up relatively quickly and cheaply. The weight of the roadway is carried by the tension of supporting cables passing over towers which receive the load of the span at the end of the bridge; the ends of the cable are anchored in the ground beyond. The supporting towers for the cables on the west side of Gilchrist's bridge most likely were of cast iron. On the eastern shore the cables were attached to high rock abutments. A nearby source of cast iron at the time was at the Starbuck Furnace in Crown Point, or their iron foundry in Troy, New York. Possibly the cast iron for the tower on the western side was shipped by rail from Troy to Gilchrist's Hudson River site.

While plans were made and components for the bridge were being assembled, a road to the river and railroad would

Map showing Washburn's Eddy, the site of Gilchrist's bridge.

The western towers of Gilchrist's bridge probably looked like this, according to Richard S. Allen.

need to be built. The rocks and boulders that covered much of the landscape would need to be removed. Laborers would be hired and teams of horses, wagons, and oxen pulling carts would haul the stones away, clearing a path.

Gilchrist's drive crossed the dirt road that led to the Harrington farm, and continued down the new road to the tracks and beyond where the bridge was built at a spot known as Washburn Eddy. The river's eddy lay behind the Washburn property—land the Major's family had leased.

On July 14, 1870, the same day Congress voted an annual pension of $3,000 to Mary Todd Lincoln, a census taker in the Town of Johnsburg listed Robert C. Gilchrist as age forty, an attorney-at-law, born in South Carolina. His personal property was listed as $2,000 and the value of his real estate as $30,000. Assessors' rolls that year valued his 'Inglewood' homestead of eighty-four acres at $500. Down the road the log cabin of Zale Harrington was valued at $50.

July can be hot in the Adirondacks but nothing like the humidity of a Charleston summer. Fields of daisies and black-eyed susans on either side of the long drive leading to the Wevertown mansion could keep little Emma busy picking bouquets for all the high-ceilinged rooms.

Maria Bowman stayed in the servant quarters at the rear of the house. She was listed on the federal census as fifty years of age, female, colored, occupation servant. Gussie's sister, seventeen-year-old Addie, was with them and could help with fifteen-month-old baby Augusta, for Gussie was pregnant again.

When they moved into the Inglewood mansion that summer in 1870, Grant was living in the White House. The fifteenth amendment giving black men the right to vote had been ratified and all eleven former Confederate states had been reorganized and readmitted to the Union. Jesse James was robbing banks in the west, and Rockefeller, sometimes called a robber baron, had incorproated the Standard Oil Company for a million dollars.

The year before, Uncle Robert had died in Fernandina, Florida, on April 29, 1869. His Charleston nephew was named executor of his uncle's will giving him more responsibilities in the north in 1870. The will read:

> "I give and devise all the rest, residue and remainder of my estate . . . to my nephew George Gilchrist and Cornelius V.S. Gilchrist and my nieces Julia K. Gilchrist and Maria C. Gilchrist children of my beloved brother John T. Gilchrist, and my nephew Robert C. Gilchrist and niece Mary Elizabeth Baker, children of my beloved sister Mary Gilchrist to be divided between them . . . share and share alike . . . and pay over annually to my said nephews and nieces any excess of income over the sum of one thousand dollars as heretofore directed to my son Ambrose and the further sum of $500 to his daughter Anna."
>
> "My earnest desire and intention in making the devices to my son and his daughter being to secure to them a maintenance and support for life and that my design shall not be defeated."

After inserting a clause stating that any attempt to bargain, sell or pledge either of the annuities would mean they would be forfeited, the will explained:

> "I most sincerely hope to convince my beloved son, Ambrose Spencer, that this executing devise is not made in any unkind feeling toward him, but in sincere and devout affection for him as my beloved son, knowing his singleness of disposition, his unfortunate connections and his liability to be deceived to his personal injury."
>
> "I most devoutly pray that my beloved son may rise in his thoughts, taking a higher rank among men and be sustained by Providence to properly appreciate my motives and cheerfully give his personal assistance."

Less than a year after his father's death, on January 14, 1870, Spencer petitioned to have his cousin execute the Deed of Trust for registered Bonds of the U.S. Government

Ambrose Spencer Gilchrist home at 130 Main Street, Warrensburg. From "A Sketchbook" by Marie H. Fisher, 1974.

bearing six percent interest for $50,000 for the payment of annuities and called for distribution according to the terms of the will.

While there were no instructions to do so, Robert bought his cousin Spencer a house at 130 Main Street, Warrensburg, a few months after his uncle's death, for $4,000. Upon Spencer's death the deed said title was to vest absolutely in his wife and any living children. The deed states, ". . . and it is further understood that the said Ambrose Spencer Gilchrist shall have an estate only as trustee in said premises not subject in law or equity to any heirs or claims of his creditors or subject to be encumbered by him."

Those restrictions and the phrase in his father's will— ". . . his unfortunate connections and his liability to be deceived to his personal injury,"—suggest doubts about Spencer's character.

Although his cousin, Robert, had bought a substantial house in Warrensburg for him, Spencer informed the *Glens Falls Messenger* that as a Civil Engineer and Surveyor of

Warrensburg, he planned to move to Glens Falls and "will open an office here about the first of May." This was also reported in the County and Vicinity News of the *Sandy Hill Herald* of April 21, 1871.

A dozen years earlier he had an advertising agency at 75 State Street in Albany. Much newspaper advertising in the nineteenth century was still promoting patent medicines, giving advertising a bad name. It's doubtful his father, a respected businessman, would have considered a career in advertising "a higher rank among men."

In addition to buying a house for Spencer, Robert paid $6,732 to each of his cousins for the inherited share of their uncle's real estate, totaling over thirty thousand dollars. He began selling the real estate he then controlled—approximately 2,500 acres sold in 1870 for $21,672. The value of an acre varied.

To John Bowman, a tannery owner in Stoney Creek, he sold 234 acres for $5,500 which may have included the necessary hemlock that tanneries required. To the blacksmith, Felix Palarand, he sold ninety-nine acres for $350.

There were other sales that year including the 1,542 acres sold to Durant on June 28th. From the hill where Gilchrist's mansion looked down on the Hudson River, he could also see the tracks of the new line and watch his suspension bridge going up.

During February 1871 a son, Robert Benjamin Gilchrist, was born to Gussie and Robert in Charleston. Newspapers that year were filled with stories of Indians on the warpath, of Temperance meetings, of the Boss Tweed ring in New York City, and of yellow fever deaths in Charleston, but for them the best news was the completion of Robert's iron bridge. It would be ready at summer's end and a picnic to celebrate the bridge's opening was planned.

Gussie's former slave, Sara Ancrum, came north with them that summer. But the family journal records that, "The climatic change being too violent for one of her temperment, jaundice which was soon engendered resulted in her death at Inglewood. . . ." They buried her with a headstone in the family plot in Wevertown where Robert's grandparents and John Thurman lay.

On September 8, 1871, nine-year-old Clarence Ross was visiting his uncle, John Loveland, on Dillon Hill. They walked to the grand opening of Gilchrist's bridge some two miles away. "The road we went was by the Anderson school house on the road between Wevertown and The Glen, turned left and went down passed the Gilchrist mansion to Washburn's Eddy where the new bridge was. In the afternoon the first locomotive came as far as this and what excitement! A steam engine and two box cars!!! What an ugly looking monster it was! What an excited, enthusiastic cheering crowd."

Some two hundred people gathered. On the bridge a table was made of boards with benches on each side the length of the bridge. There were speeches and resolutions passed, but what impressed little Clarence Ross were the champagne bottles on the picnic table.

Apparently there was a misunderstanding about 'the picnic.' In a letter written to Ella Spoor by her Aunt Ann, she wrote, "Now I must not forget to tell you there was a great picnic on the suspension bridge the day after we were there. There was some mistake about the entertainment. Each trusted the other to provide and so did not have any. I suppose good speeches made up the deficiency."

The Ross boy added to his story: "Through some misunderstanding everyone thought he was going to furnish 'the eats' so no one took anything, but when they got there they realized there had been a misunderstanding for all there was there was a bushel of boiled potatoes, a boiled ham and a dozen bottles of champagne. Well, I put in a very strenuous day and was I hungry when I got home and completely exhausted."

The Glens Falls Republican called it "A Wire Bridge Across the Hudson" and described it as "being 15 feet wide, with a span of 230 feet, constructed by Charles MacDonald of 80 Broadway, New York, of the pattern known as Roebling's bridges, . . . and is a most substantial structure."

Town of Johnsburg   Town of Chester

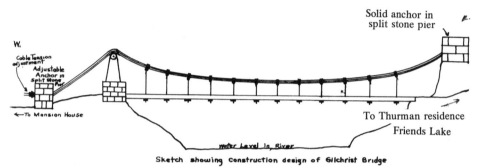

Sketch by Tennyson Baldwin showing construction design of
Gilchrist Bridge.

The article ended saying, "The following resolutions
were unanimously passed at a large and enthusiastic meeting held on the bridge:

RESOLVED, That the town Supervisors, Trustees
and Road Commissioners be requested to take the
necessary means for putting the road between Wevertown and the Bridge in good traveling condition without delay, and also to grade the approach to the west
end of the Bridge, so communication between Wevertown and Chestertown may be had at an early day.

RESOLVED, That the Adirondack Company be
informed that the terms of the agreement required by
them is or soon will be complied with: that the Bridge is
completed, and the road connected therewith will also
be completed in about three weeks and they are there-
fore requested to establish their depot at this point as
already promised by them at an early day."

Those resolutions probably were part of Robert's

speech to the crowd that early September day. Some towns-people walked to the bridge as young Clarence Ross did, others hitched up their wagons or buggies to travel to the grand opening. Social gatherings and speeches provided entertainment in their hard-working lives—and there was the iron horse to be seen!

After the day's excitement, with the outside sound of crickets that signaled the end of summer, and the children put to bed, Gussie and Robert would have a chance to talk over all that happened that day.

With their old-fashioned decency and sense of duty they might have wondered if they were out of step with the locals. There was the mixup about the food. But more than that Robert must have been unwillingly aware of the disquieting turn his fortunes had taken. He could read about it in *The Glens Falls Republican* the next week in a letter to the editor following the account of his bridge's opening.

Signed with the initials G.L.S., it said:

> "Any one reading some of the papers would suppose that it is all a wilderness north of the large village of Chester—but there are a few settlers in Pottersville, Millbrook, Schroon, North Hudson, etc. And the businessmen of those places, together with a few at Chester, have formed a company called the Central Bridge Co. and are building a wire bridge costing $15,000 across the Hudson at Folsom's Landing (some three miles above Mr. Gilchrist's bridge), that being the most central place on the Adirondack railroad for the above named towns and Johnsburgh. . . . Mr. Gilchrist has got a bridge built, but he has got to dig through a mountain of granite before he can have a road to get on to the bridge from the Chester side of the river."

Gilchrist's would be the first suspension bridge across the Hudson River, but now he had competition for a depot.

CHAPTER TEN

The Other Bridge

Before there was a bridge to shorten the distance to Chester, Jonathan Folsom established a ferry crossing some three miles north of Washburn Eddy where the river is shallow and tranquil. He owned land on either side of the Hudson, and to settlers pushing north through the territory, the crossing became known as Folsom's Landing.

Local businessmen believed this was the better place for a bridge across the Hudson. And if the Adirondack Railway granted them a depot, it would guarantee income from tolls the bridge could charge departing passengers who wished to cross.

For president of the newly organized Folsom Landing Central Bridge Company, Edwin A. Bush was chosen. He owned the "Ellen," a steamship that traveled Schroon Lake bringing tourists to the surrounding hotels and cottages. Three directors of the newly formed Central Bridge Company lived in the village of Schroon Lake. One of these men was James Leland.

An Adirondack Railway brochure related that, "The Leland House at Schroon Lake Village is located upon the rising lake shore at a point which commands a view of nearly the entire lake. . . . this favorite house is conducted by Messrs. L. R. & E. D. Locke of Pottersville." E. D. Locke was a director and secretary of the Folsom Landing Central Bridge Company.

Locke and his son, Lorenzo, owned the Pottersville Hotel. ". . . its principal business in providing dinners for guests bound to and from the resorts around Schroon Lake and farther north and west." The two Lockes bought eight shares of bridge stock.

David Aldrich, another director bought $1,000 worth of stock. His boarding house at the Central Bridge site housed the railroad workers bringing the tracks north. Elected to the New York State Assembly in 1866, it was Aldrich who introduced legislation for a Glens Falls monument to those in the north who died in the Civil War.

The next largest stockholder after David Aldrich was John W. Armstrong who bought twenty-four shares in the Central Bridge for $600. *The Glens Falls Republican* of September 3, 1872, announced that "Mr. John W. Armstrong has established an express between Johnsburgh, Wevertown and Riverside on the Adirondack Railroad for the accomodation of passengers and freight." These were the men interested in seeing that tourists continued on north and who intended to capture their share of that trade.

Once the company raised eight thousand dollars by selling stock at $25 a share, the townspeople of Schroon Lake voted to sell municipal bonds "and the moneys arising from the sale thereof by the supervisor, for the time being, of the said town of Schroon, shall be paid over to the treasurer of the said Folsom Landing Bridge Company, for the purpose of completing said bridge and no other. . . ." The town of Schroon bought $4,000 worth of bridge stock.

Chapter 853 of New York State law was passed on April 6, 1871, "to legalize the acts of the tax-payers of the town of Schroon in relation to their subscription to the capital stock of said company." Just how important the bridge was seen as bringing business to their village was revealed in the town's willingness to tax themselves to cover interest on the bonds.

Of the more than seventy individuals who purchased stock in the bridge at Riverside, most listed residences in the small towns not far from the bridge. One share for $25

Riverside Bridge, looking east. The hanging sign reads,
"For crossing this bridge faster than a walk $10 penalty."

was bought by a Mr. Mendleson with no residence listed but
following his name, in brackets, was the word peddler.

Built in 1872, the Central Bridge with its wooden
towers at each end, had a span of 308 feet and was ten feet
wide. Its cement foundations came to the highwater mark,
crucial as the river rose from spring flooding. Fears that ice
breaking up would take out the bridge caused a man to stay
in the tower at night to watch during a spring thaw.

Businessmen like E.D. Locke, James Leland, and
Edwin Bush who wanted to keep tourists coming to Schroon
Lake, also saw the bridge tolls as returning a profit for its
investors. The company charged three cents to walk across.
To lead a horse cost five cents, ten cents for a one-horse rig,
fifteen cents for a team and thirty cents for a 'tally-ho' or
stagecoach. John Kipp drove the stage that picked up
departing train passengers headed for the northern resorts
and lived, with his wife, Mattie, by the bridge. She became
the tolltaker.

Those who got off at Riverside Station on the western

Courtesy of Lewis Waddell
The Riverside stage met passengers and freight at the railway depot.

shore, the last stop before the end of the line at North Creek, could be met by stagecoach and taken across the bridge to Chestertown, but also to points north. Beyond Pottersville and Schroon Lake there was Blue Mountain Lake, Racquette Lake and the Great Camps.

On the eastern shore of the river, ten acres had been deeded in 1868 to the Johnsburg Methodists for their Riverside Camp meeting grounds where people could gather to listen to sermons. Some drove loaded hay wagons to the grounds just for the day, and after they hitched their horses to the grove of trees, gathered with basket lunches. Those who came greater distances brought tents in order to spend longer time.

Trees were cleared for a place of worship, which at first was only a small platform with a roof over it. Worshippers sat outdoors on tree stumps. While the ministers believed it was a way to propagate the faith for the worshippers, there was also the attraction of a social gathering as a scattered mountain people assembled.

The Glens Falls Republican, at the end of the summer
in 1874, reported that "The camp-meeting at Riverside,
which closed Wednesday, was one of the largest ever held in
this part of the country. There were seventy-three tents
erected, of all manner of materials and style, and for the
past week the grove where the meeting was held has presented a very pretty as well as lively appearance."

As riders on horseback, farm wagons loaded with children, and two-seater buckboards passed through Wevertown on the way to the campgrounds, youngsters like
Pauline Davison stood in her front yard and waved to the
parade of people passing by.

The newspaper reported, "A large crowd was present
on the ground Sunday, the numbers being estimated at
from three to five thousand people. . . . The circle of tents
had to be made larger, and then many were obliged to put
up their tents behind the outer circle, and in some places
they were three deep." Not only did people come by wagons
and buggies, there were trains run on the Adirondack railroad from both ways, "and both trains were loaded down."

There is no record of what Gilchrist's thoughts or
doubts were about the bridge he built or of the competing
Central Bridge with its newly acquired Riverside Depot.
What is documented in Deed Book 26 at the Warren County
records is a Gilchrist sale to Origin Vandenburgh of 5,299
acres in consideration of the sum of certain exchange of real
estate and $10.00, ". . . being the property descended to
party of the first part from the estate of John Thurman."

Origin Vandenburgh was an attorney from Syracuse
and one of the first to recommend the construction of an
underground railroad in New York City. "In 1868 when
leading citizens of this city united in the move before the
Legislature for the passage of an act incorporating a company and authorizing the construction of an underground
road, Senator Folger and other Senators from the interior
insisted that, inasmuch as Mr. Vandenburgh was the
original promoter, his rights should be recognized in the
bill. . . . This incident gave to Mr. Vandenburgh the title of

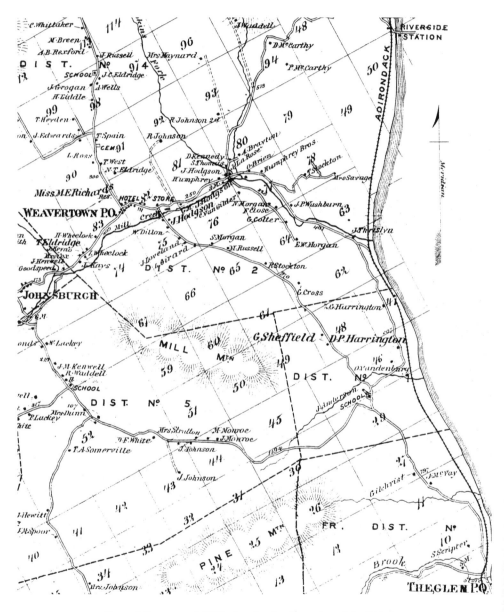

Beers Atlas map of 1876 showing land purchased by Origin
Vandenburg.

'Original' Vandenburgh, by which he was known and called both here and in Albany."

Perhaps realizing he would forever be the outsider affected Robert's decision to sell to Vandenburgh. Perhaps there were doubts the road to Chester on the eastern side of his bridge could ever be built, or his decision to sell out came when Riverside was granted a depot by their bridge.

Whatever the reason, Robert and Gussie, on November 23, 1872, hardly more than a year since their bridge picnic, conveyed to Origin Vandenburgh, land that included their Inglewood mansion. The lengthy deed listing lot numbers and acreage also included lot "twenty nine (29) three hundred and four (304) acres including the Wire Suspension Bridge and franchises connected therewith. . . ."

Vandenburgh's interest in a subway for New York City may have extended to the railroad in the Adirondacks, but there is no evidence that he ever did anything with the bridge or mansion. Old postcards depicted the Central Bridge with its thirty-foot towers and the words "Only Suspension Bridge on Hudson River." By the time their bridge was finished they could say that. When Gilchrist sold to Vandenburgh in 1872 his bridge was standing. A map of the railroads of the State of New York from the *Annual Report of the New York State Engineer and Surveyor for 1882* also shows a stop at Washburn's Eddy.

For the next twenty years following his purchase of the iron bridge and Inglewood, Vandenburgh's priority was getting a subway built in New York City. At one time the former Union general, George McClellan, was his company's president. In May 1883, needing funds to carry on his subway project, Origin Vandenburgh sold most of the land he bought from Gilchrist in 1872 to Andrew Thruston and William Parker, lumbermen from Chester.

Gilchrist returned in 1872 to live in Charleston, the year their last daughter, Annie, was born. There was still family land to sell in the Adirondacks. Deeds show that he appeared in the north with Gussie at some of the sales. There is no evidence of any bitterness in light of what he accomplished after returning to the south. However, as he read or heard of what was going on in the Adirondacks he must have been disappointed at his lack of success in what he rightly saw as possibilities for commercial development.

On April 1, 1873, like a cruel April Fool's joke, heavy, wet snow damaged the bridge Gilchrist had built. A week later a small item with a Johnsburgh dateline in *The Glens Falls Republican* said, "On the 1st inst. one of the anchorages of the suspension bridge at Washburn's Eddy gave way, and the bridge now hangs suspended by one cable, bottom side up." The unknown newspaper writer offered his view of why. "The weight of snow and careless manner in which the anchorages were built is the cause. The bridge was erected by Mr. R. C. Gilchrist some year and a half ago, and cost upwards of $8,000.

One local story said Gilchrist had wanted a boulder removed from the road to make a straight approach to the bridge. Some theorized the blast that took out the boulder may have weakened the bridge. Charles MacDonald, engineer of Gilchrist's bridge, went on to build bigger, more important bridges, although his name is never associated with the Inglewood Bridge in any of his papers. Nor is there any record of the bridge in the Gibbes-Gilchrist papers in Charleston.

Along with the newspaper accounts of scarlet fever prevailing in the mountains that spring were news items of other damage done by the heavy snow and ice. "Two bridges on The Glen creek, one on the Johnsburgh road, were carried off by the high water on the 30th ult." Another said, "The ice in the Hudson broke up on the 31st ult., about two miles above The Glen, and moving out, dammed up again about a mile below."

From the nearby town of Thurman came word, "The snow previous to the recent thaw was full four feet deep, the traveled roads being higher than the top of the fences." A week later the same paper reported, "A temporary bridge has been erected at The Glen on the Johnsburgh road, in place of the one carried away by the freshet. The mail is

Postcard showing "Fulson" Landing Bridge, Riparius, formerly Riverside.

Photograph by Wes Pelkey

Remaining segments of cable that anchored Gilchrist's suspension bridge.

again running regularly three times a week."

Once the ice broke up, logging drives could begin. The paper said, "The beautiful snow is fast passing away here. Mill Creek is up to good driving pitch and the annual run of logs will soon commence." Mill Creek empties into the Hudson just above where Gilchrist's bridge stood. If his bridge was hanging bottom side up by one or two cables, the lumbermen would need to cut what remained to clear a passageway. The rushing spring waters would carry it away.

Another summer when they came north to sell land, Robert and Gussie may have driven down the road in a rented buggy to see what remained of abutments and cables. David Noble, postmaster of Wevertown, who notorized the deeds indicating they had appeared before him in person, may have told them what happened. They may even have paid ten cents for a one-horse rig to cross the bridge at Riverside to Chester.

Meanwhile the Adirondack Railway's brochure praised "the excellence of the passenger service, both by rail and stage . . . to tempt city people of wealth and taste to come to Schroon year after year, and the pretty cottages many of them have built, peep out from the foliage as we speed along the smooth blue lake."

The commercial development of the northern mountains continued in the way Gilchrist envisioned, but the local men who promoted the bridge at Riverside were the beneficiaries. The thoughtful and reserved Southerner whose speech sounded so strange to a mountain people, turned instead to another kind of bridge building. Reconstruction in the South was going on and Gilchrist would make his contribution there.

CHAPTER ELEVEN

Back in Charleston

Moderate men like Robert C. Gilchrist were needed in a region divided by factions during the social and political dislocation called Reconstruction. While the black freedmen briefly enjoyed new liberties and opportunities, the resentment of whites who felt threatened by the loss of power surfaced in groups like the Redeemers who distrusted both freedmen and poor whites. They sought in the 1870's to restore the privileges the antebellum white man of wealth once held.

Letters exchanged between Uncle Robert and his nephew immediately after the war revealed their concern for what was happening. His uncle wrote, "I think I stated in a former letter that our papers and their correspondents did as much, or more, than southern papers to keep up and get up a bad political feeling."

"The 'Dignity' you speak of is considered arrogance— and produces many articles like the article I enclose." The clipping he sent reported a speech of Senator Wilson in Boston to the New England Anti-Slavery society.

Wilson said: "South Carolina had $400,000,000 of property when the war commenced—$200,000,000 of it in slaves. All gone — their railroads worn out — their banks failed — the poorest civilized community on God's earth today. We Republicans can carry that state this Autumn by from 20,000 to 30,000 majority and hold it. (Applause.) I was told by an ex-Governor of the State, referring to a district where Slavery was the strongest, that such was the strength of our principles and our organization that there would not be a candidate run against us for Congress. . . ."

Uncle Robert expressed his opinion. "Cold — party article — utterly devoid of any sympathy. As I before wrote you—the Carolina Dignity spurning friend and foe alike— has helped to produce the very thing you complain of and probably the result Senator Wilson spouts."

Their correspondence included reactions to what they read. He wrote his nephew, "I am not surprised that Deforest should write a book of as little merit and as much malignity as the criticism (if it may be so called). I never took *any* fancy to the man. . . . You always thought him a small potato—and is of the class I fear you are long to be cursed with. I sincerely wish you were elsewhere than in C. Probably there may be a brighter day after the next election but while the present generation and feeling lasts—it cannot be."

Newspapers of the period were fiercely partisan, with little separation between news and editorial content. In the north *The Glens Falls Republican*, which decried the Republican party and supported the Democrats, had an article May 21, 1872 with the heading, "The Misgoverned South," which read:

> "A lady resident of Charleston, writing a private letter to a friend in Washington, paints this picture of Radical rule as administerd by Grant's satraps in the Sunny South."
>
> "'Our political state becomes worse and worse. Our Governor is a robber. Our Legislature is made up of negroes who can't sign their names, and adventurers who can't go home for fear of the penitentiary. They steal openly. . . . make laws to hedge themselves round from justice. The jails are filled to overflowing with the innocent, while murderers, houseburners, and hardened thieves go about in open daylight, unpunished. The taxes are doubled and trebled to keep

up the state of thievish officials and their negro mis-
tresses. To own property is a curse. To be a negro is a
blessing, but to be a negro rascal is the greatest of all
blessings. To be white and honest is the sure road to
ruin and despair. What a fanciful satire to call this a
free government and the present a state of profound
peace."

But Gilchrist stated his belief:

"The trouble is with the people not with the
place. The 'Bourbons' have suffered greatly and will
suffer more unless they conform to the new order. It is
the old cry against machinery and those who will sit
down and wring their hands instead of using them in
other work will grow poorer."
"Everything in Charleston has changed and is
changing, and those who will keep in the old ruts are
being run over by the new element in the community.
I have great faith in Charleston."

Gilchrist rejoined the Washington Light Infantry he
first joined in 1849; his father had once been its commander. One writer told of Gilchrist's father's command
during the intense nullification excitement in the years of
1830 to 1832: "Being a Union man he was proscribed politically and socially, and when he accepted from President
Jackson the office of United States District Attorney, four-
fifths of the Washington Light Infantry resigned. Capt.
Gilchrist ordered a parade of the corps at that time and
marched through the streets with more men in the band
than in ranks. In a few months, however, another parade
showed more men in line than ever before in the history of
the corps."

The same writer described the rebirth of the corps. "At
the close of the war, when South Carolina was literally the
'prostrate state,' military satraps, carpetbaggers and igno-
rant negroes dominating our people, when an armed white
volunteer militia was forbidden, recourse was had to private
'rifle clubs,' with sporting rifles for arms. . . ." which were

"in fact, politico-military organizations." These rifle clubs eventually became the National Rifle Association in 1871.

Joining the W.L.I. as a second lieutenant in 1873, Gilchrist was elected to first lieutenant the following spring. In a later testimonial his participation was praised. "There are many senior members who will quickly recall the change in the Rifle Club from a non-military to a military condition; how the first copies of Upton's Tactics were brought from New York for the instruction of the Washington Light Infantry, how he prepared sixty members (in thirty drills of one hour each) for the Bunker Hill parade in Boston, 17th June, 1875, and how the command was cheered along miles of march for its soldierly appearance and accurate drill."

The invitation to march with former enemies only ten years after war's end was the direct result of what Gilchrist had done the year before. The Washington Light Infantry planned an Easter Fair to benefit the widows and orphans of dead veterans of the Charleston unit and invited the militia units of Boston to participate.

"A number of items were sent from Boston to be sold or raffled at the fair, and the surgeon of the First Regiment of Massachusetts Militia and a former commander of the Boston Light Infantry, with their wives, came to Charleston to preside over the Boston table. With appropriate ceremonies, Captain John K. Hall of Boston presented a flag bearing the blended coats of arms of Massachusetts and South Carolina to the Washington Light Infantry."

Spring in Charleston is one of the best seasons to visit the city. Although parts of the city destroyed by the great fire of 1861 and war's shelling had not been rebuilt, there were flowering peach trees in blossom, lush fuchsia azaleas and yellow jasmine to soften the city's image.

The fair was a joyous occasion with booths and lights and milling crowds. The artist Gilchrist designed the decorations for the great hall where the fair was held. One visitor wrote, "No such scene has ever been witnessed in Charleston before or since. It captivated the public and after the first night the hall was so crowded as to impede moving about.

The large sum of eight thousand dollars was realized and by judicious investments and reinvestments has grown to fifteen thousand dollars—the income annually distributed to the families of members who served in the war and have passed away—the only permanent Confederate charity fund in the South."

The warmth of the Charleston welcome resulted in an invitation to the Washington Light Infantry to go to Boston the following year. Opinion was divided about going, and the time to prepare was short. But the Adirondack bridge-builder in command of the Washington Light Infantry was more successful in building bridges between former enemies. Along with a unit from Virginia, the W.L.I. left to participate in the Bunker Hill Centennial celebration. There were fifty-four officers and men sent with a state flag from South Carolina's Governor Chamberlain, a Yale law graduate, to carry to Massachusetts.

Chamberlain sent the flag "as proof of my personal and official interest in their organization, and especially in the purposes and feelings which inspire their present visit to Massachusetts." From the Battery came a thirty-seven gun salute as the steamer carrying the unit sailed out of Charleston Harbor.

Arriving in New York City they were greeted by the Old Guard unit. The two militias paraded through crowds of spectators and, after a breakfast at Delmonico's, left together for Boston with the accompanying band playing proudly. According to the *Boston Post*, it was the first appearance of a unit made up of those who fought for the Confederacy on their city streets, but Bostonians happily greeted the representatives of a sister state.

The hours of marching and drills of the Washington Light Infantry with Gilchrist revealed their military conditioning and caused the crowd to believe they were in fact the pet company of Charleston, composed of the 'flower of its young men.' They stepped smartly in their blue-coated uniforms with gilt ball buttons, white trousers and white gloves. On their heads were dark blue caps with a border of leopard skin and red pompom. Cheering spectators convinced them of their welcome and that by-gones were indeed by-gones.

The next day the Infantry unit was welcomed by Massachusetts Governor William Gaston. The Charleston speaker presented him with a palmetto cane, and referred to Governor Chamberlain's attempts to carry out a reform program saying, "We cannot forget that, when our State was plunged deepest in the mire of corruption and degradation, Massachusetts, by one of her sons, gave us the helping hand, and is now lifting our Government from a state of obloquy to something of republicanism."

Good feelings established in New York and Boston continued when the Boston Light Infantry accepted an invitation to Charleston the next year for the anniversary celebration of the Battle of Fort Moultrie. Patriotic speeches were given by both sides. At the Academy of Music Colonel William L. Trenholm said, ". . . if this occasion is happily instrumental in promoting a better understanding between the sections, it will have accomplished its purpose and vindicated its claim to nationality."

The Commander of the host Infantry then acknowledged the gift from Boston, and commented on past differences and present strides toward unity:

> "You have brought with you a pine severed from
> its roots in Massachusetts and placed it beside our
> own Palmetto. . . . As we march beneath the entwined
> branches of these emblems of two states as extreme in
> their political faith as their geographical position, let
> us (remember) the pledge we made at Bunker Hill
> that henceforth there shall be no sectional strife but
> that we will hold that man or party as a common
> enemy who by word or act shall disturb the harmony,
> mutual confidence and good will that should bind
> together every portion of this great country."

The applause that followed could only be heartening to the son who had always been a Unionist, forever trying to reconcile the two regions of his heritage. Commander Gilchrist continued:

> "A year ago we met for the first time on your own soil, but the feeling that we were strangers soon melted in the warmth of greeting and a generous hospitality which made us realize that however the honest differences of opinion we each entertained, had separated us in the past."

Reminding his audience they met together now as citizens of a common country and joint heirs of the same proud heritage, he said,

> "We have therefore looked forward with pleasure to this day when we could greet you at our own homes and beneath the foliage of our own palmetto. . . ."

Public eloquence on a momentous occasion in 1876 called for stirring words and Gilchrist met the challenge.

> "Twelve months ago we gathered around America's consecrated shrine and joined with the vast multitude assembled at Bunker Hill to do reverence to those brave men who struck the first blow for our freedom and laid broad the foundations of our republic."
> "Tomorrow we will stand upon the spot where our fathers a hundred years ago bid defiance to the greatest naval power in the world, and with but thirty guns relying only on the justice of their cause and the strong arm of the God of battles beat back the fleet of British vessels and won for America the first victory of the Revolution."

Gilchrist then turned to how important this joining of North and South was:

> "But Comrades, to us, this meeting has a deeper significance still."

"As the representative soldiery of the three great sections of the 'old thirteen,' the Eastern, middle and southern states—we here rendezvous for our march to the cradle of American Independence to celebrate our nation's birthday, and there at the great Centennial at Philadelphia, marching in solid column with those who will come from beyond the Green Mountains of New England, the beautiful waters of the Hudson and Potomac, the forest of the Carolinas and the savannahs of Georgia, under gallant Generals who 'ere now commanded both 'the blue and the grey,' we will show to the assembled myriads of the nation gathered from her remotest bounds, that we have buried the animosities of the war, and as true soldiers honoring each others courage, respecting each others motives, harboring no resentments, and forgetting all that is to be forever in the past, we now meet as 'brothers in arms' henceforth one in heart. . . ."

The "rendezvous to march to the Cradle of American Independence" meant militia from New York, Massachusetts, and Georgia would leave Charleston together with Gilchrist's Washington Light Infantry. Mayor Courtenay and Gilchrist had proposed the idea to have one military unit from each of the original thirteen states march together in the 1876 Philadelphia Centennial parade. On the Union's one hundredth birthday, the South would be there.

CHAPTER TWELVE

Eighteen Hundred Seventy-Six

Every hamlet, town, and city in 1876 was ready to observe the Fourth of July in its own way. All over America the country was preparing to celebrate one hundred years of independence from England with parades, picnics, fireworks, speeches, and everywhere draping the familiar red, white and blue bunting. It was a national birthday all sections of the country could share.

Philadelphia, the birthplace of Independence, planned for months to celebrate the event with the first major international exposition on a 236-acre site. President Grant officially opened the doors through which eight million paying customers eventually passed to see the 180 pavilions' offerings at the Centennial Exposition. Every kind of entertainment, amusement and information was included. Most popular of all was the Great Machinery Hall.

People waited in long lines and once inside could see the Roebling display with its sample section of cable for the Brooklyn Bridge. In the days Gilchrist spent in Philadelphia with his Washington Light Infantry, the great hall would be a priority visit. With its steam engines, turbines, and inventions, there was much to attract the boy inventor who built a prize winning steam engine so long ago.

Each of these centennials offered a chance for reconciliation and mutual respect for former enemies. It was the Washington Light Infantry's invitation to help Charleston's widows and orphans which first opened the way. Now at Philadelphia all animosities seemed forgotten in the cheers that greeted Gilchrist's unit as they paraded through the city streets.

> "The idea of a Centennial Legion, composed of one military unit from each of the original thirteen states, had been proposed in July 1875 by William A. Courtenay and Captain Robert C. Gilchrist, the commanding officer of the Washington Light Infantry, and the idea had received support in Boston and New York. . . .
>
> "According to the Philadelphia *Press*, the Centennial Legion was the 'most attractive and interesting portion of the whole parade' on July 4th, and the feature 'that the public generally had been looking forward to for months.' The Washington Light Infantry was the color company. They were carrying the Eutaw flag, and their appearance was 'the occasion of a spontaneous outburst of applause from the assembled multitude.'"

In spite of the good feelings the Charleston unit enjoyed in Philadelphia, they returned home to angry voices and violent clashes as the 1876 elections neared. The Democratic party had nominated the popular Samuel Tilden, reform governor of New York, as their presidential candidate. The Republicans nominated Ohio's governor, Rutherford B. Hayes. Hayes' honest administrations in Ohio convinced the party it had the right man to defuse charges of corruption prevailing in Grant's presidency.

Tilden won by a large popular vote but lacked a majority in the electoral college. The disputed election resulted when two sets of electoral votes were sent to Congress from several states, including South Carolina. Riots broke out in Charleston when both candidates for governor of South Carolina claimed victory.

In a testimonial to Gilchrist, he was given credit for his quick response. "It was during his command of the Rifle

Club that the great political revolution took place in South Carolina and the great election riot of November, 1876, occurred in Charleston. It is a matter of proper pride to this corps to record the fact that the first rifle club armed and equipped that was at the point of danger, in season for active duty, was Major Gilchrist's command, with eighty rifles, arriving on the ground in advance of the companies of United States troops then on duty at this port."

The disputed presidential election was settled by an electoral commission which after some negotiation gave the prize to the Republican Hayes. Representatives of Hayes, with the consent of Southern Democrats, struck a bargain that federal troops would be withdrawn, ending Reconstruction in fact.

The newly elected President believed public opinion had changed. "Some years after he left the White House, Hayes told Mayor William A. Courtenay of Charleston that the warm reception given the Washington Light Infantry of Charleston at the Bunker Hill Centennial celebration in 1875 had made it possible for him to support the government of (Democrat) Wade Hampton, instead of that of the Republican claimant, Daniel H. Chamberlain."

Wade Hampton, a popular antebellum aristocrat, had originally opposed secession, but like Gilchrist chose his state when war was inevitable. As governor he advocated decent treatment for former slaves, won a second term, and went on to serve in the United States Senate.

The year 1876 with all its centennial celebration and election riot excitement, also brought great sadness to the Gilchrist family. On April 29th, Gussie's mother, Anne Roper Gibbes died. On July 29th, their baby daughter, Elizabeth, died only fourteen days after birth. The cause of death given was 'premature at seven months.'

Two years earlier the family moved to a much larger home at 12 Bee Street, on the corner of Ashley, just around the corner from their former frame house at 27 Rutledge Avenue. The beautiful red brick house was large enough for the four children and Gussie's spinster sister, Addie.

Photograph by Wes Pelkey

Home of Robert and Gussie, 12 Bee Street, Charleston, as it appears today.

MAP OF HISTORIC CHARLESTON

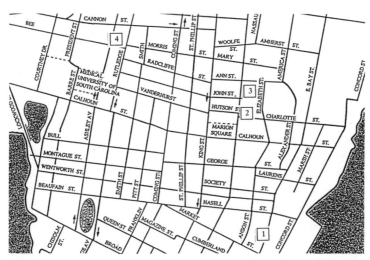

Courtesy of Robert N. Rosen

1. 245 East Bay Street;   2. Second Presbyterian Church;
3. 4 John Street;   4. 12 Bee Street

The three-story Greek Revival mansion had been bought in trust for Gussie for $8,500 on June 9, 1874. Four years later an additional strip of land was added to the east of the house. Described as a splendid specimen of a Charleston double house with a wide central hall and stairway, each floor had wide white-columned porches extending on the south side to capture the harbor breezes.

Gilchrist continued his law practice in Charleston throughout that decade and continued to sell small parcels of land in the north. He also used wood from the Adirondacks in the headquarters of the Washington Light Infantry. One writer said:

> "The want of an armory and headquarters had long been felt with the restoration to a recognized military position. On Governor Hampton's assuming the Executive office of the State, in the spring of 1877 a committee was appointed to consider how the company's want could be supplied. A negotiation was begun with the officers of the Grand Lodge of Masons for an alteration of the main hall, which ended satisfactorily.
>
> "The plans for their change were prepared by Major Gilchrist and successfully executed. The interior was finished in hard wood brought from his property in the Adirondacks and is as beautiful and perfect . . . as when first completed. The magnificent walnut gun cases, with rack for one hundred and twenty rifles."

Gilchrist resigned his command in the Washington Light Infantry in 1877, possibly to have time to write his account of the defense of Morris Island.

Writing would soon be aided by the invention of a typewriting machine. On exhibit in 1874 in Rochester, it printed only in capital letters with a carriage return operated by a foot pedal. More likely Gilchrist set pen to paper as he began his recollection of what it was like to defend Morris Island during the summer of 1863. Around this time Mary

Boykin Chesnut, too, began writing a book based on her wartime diaries.

Gilchrist's "The Defense of Morris Island" was published in the *Charleston Yearbook of 1884*. The scholarly essay contained maps, drawings, lists of casualties, lists of those who shared in its defense, and a few short profiles. What Gilchrist experienced is vividly described, and credit for bravery given to others.

His college friend, Paul Hamilton Hayne, wrote to him for permission to quote from it in *The Southern Bivouac*. In one letter to Hayne, Gilchrist answered a number of questions and indicated he had checked with Chichester to substantiate what he remembered.

In his introduction to the *Bivouac* article, the poet Hayne reflected:

> "Had some shrewd Gitana ventured to foretell in our 'salad days' the sort of reputation which Gilchrist was destined to win, there is no doubt she would have been laughed to scorn.
>
> "And yet, *au fond* there was wild, hot blood, blood of the born soldier, in this quiet young man's veins. He inherited a gallant and determined temper from his English ancestors, especially from his grandfathers Adam and Robert Gilchrist. . . . Thus, after all, nothing could have been more natural by the law of heredity than their descendant's martial conduct when his section and State were threatened by Federal invasion.
>
> "Though but a lieutenant, he commanded this company all through the protracted and terrible siege, and his name deserves to be handed down to posterity as one of its truest heroes.
>
> "Scarcely of the medium height, pale, thin, and delicate of aspect, so exceptional, still, was the resiliency of his constitution, backed by a strong soul, that he out-labored and out-wore not a few of the most vigorous looking men in the garrison. Active, observant, constantly at his post by day and by night, it is clear that a description of the battle of Fort Wagner

and the momentous incidents which accompanied and followed it could not have fallen into better hands."

Hayne had received a copy of the *Charleston Yearbook for 1884* and said:

> "It is an essay carefully prepared, and rife with material beyond price to the future historian. When in years to come the Xenophon or Thucydides shall arise commissioned to write of the great secession contest, he will doubtless be led by his beneficent Muse to consult among other memorabilia this lucid and truthful narrative.
>
> "I have the author's permission to use his facts; he consents, good reader, to be your guide and mine through a labyrinth of somewhat devious events, and to show us the different phases of one of the sternest and grandest acts in the tragedy of modern warfare."

Gilchrist's friend then proceeded to quote from the essay and embellish the narrative in his own flamboyant style. Revealing his never-abandoned views of the inferiority of the former slaves, Hayne described the attack of the Massachusetts 54th, portrayed a century later in the movie "Glory."

> "And conspicuous in the van, on came the little misguided and unfortunate Massachusetts Colonel Shaw, his long hair waving behind him, as he led his sable *enfants perdus*."

Hayne editorialized,

> ". . . this pusillanimity of 'the Black Regiment,' by the side of which even the action of the Spartan Helots (who confronted bravely enough their masters' spears, and cowered only at the crack of the whip) looks like loftiest heroism; then a grand deed, what the old Northmen would have called a deed of *derring-do*, was performed by men of the ever dominant Caucasian race. . . ."

Nothing like that is in Gilchrist's article. He chose to use the words of another to describe the 54th Massachusetts and quoted Judge Cowley's account from "Life Alfoat and Ashore." ". . . on approaching the ditch they broke; the greater part of them followed their intrepid Colonel, bounded over the ditch, mounted the parapet, and planted their flag in the most gallant manner upon the ramparts, where Shaw was shot dead; while the rest were seized with a furious panic, and acted like wild beasts let loose from a menagerie."

It is the only time Gilchrist used the words of another in his long account of the defense of Morris. Nowhere is there evidence of racism on the part of Gilchrist. His father opposed slavery. Gussie and he buried the former slave, Sara Ancrum, who came north with them in 1871, in the family plot with his grandparents in Wevertown.

Hayne ended his review of Gilchrist's essay by reminding the reader that ". . . One who visits Morris Island today will vainly search for a solitary fragment of the grand old Confederate earth-work. The winds, with unseen, ethereal fingers, have twisted up the former foundations, and with stormy breath have blown the ancient boundaries afar. The ocean also is not idle. . . ."

When Gilchrist received a copy of the *Bivouac* article he answered in a letter to Hayne, "I thank you for your flattering notice of me personally and for your friendly appreciation of my work. You have far surpassed the original. While in my account I gave solid facts and an unvarnished tale, you have dressed it in such vivid pen painting that one can participate in the strife, realizing, but not sharing, the danger."

They exchanged several letters until Hayne's death in 1886. Gilchrist's letters at times revealed his thoughts on what was going on in Charleston after Reconstruction. In that decade two natural disasters hit Charleston. In another letter—this time to his sister—he wrote about the one in 1885 which nearly cost him his life.

CHAPTER THIRTEEN

The One Before Hugo

No longer traveling to the Adirondacks to spend summers, the Gilchrist family spent holidays and vacations at a second home on Sullivan Island, one of the barrier islands protecting Charleston's harbor. Before a bridge was built over the Cooper River, the island was reached by ferries.

Even the family pet, Pippo, left the hot and humid city when the family went to their summer home on Sullivan Island where the little dog could run on the beach after the children. In the summer of 1885 the children were fast becoming adolescents. Little Gussie wasn't so little anymore at sixteen, and Robbie turned fourteen on his last birthday, Annie thirteen. The extended family included Emma, unmarried at twenty-two and still living at home, and Gussie's sister, Addie.

Their large, two-story wooden house near the beach had a steep, overhanging slate roof. The orange trees and the big magnolia provided shade from the blistering summer sun. But on August 24, 1885, the official weather forecast for the South Atlantic states called for local rains.

Robert and Gussie had a guest that evening. In a letter to his sister, Mary Elizabeth Baker, he told her, "On Monday night Maria Budd took tea with us. We had a pleasant evening and about ten I saw her home to the Moultrie house." As Gilchrist walked back along the beach under a full moon, there were some clouds and a brisk wind he

Courtesy of the South Carolina Historical Society
Gilchrist summer home on Sullivan Island.

found not unpleasant.

Gussie was waiting up for him although the others had gone to bed. They retired, too, and slept soundly until four in the morning. Gilchrist wrote what happened next. "Gussie then awoke and looked out to see that a storm was brewing. As she was anxious I got up and dressed. The moon enabled us to see about us."

Back in the city a violent thunderstorm with heavy rain and winds out of the southeast battered the city shortly after midnight. Rain stopped by morning but the winds increased and began to damage the city's roofs and trees. Slates and tree limbs began falling into the streets.

By 5 a.m. Gussie and Robert on Sullivan Island were looking out the upstairs bedroom window, and ". . . looking towards the beach saw the first wave sweep over the barrier of sand that is high water mark." High tide came at 7 a.m. so it still had two hours to rise. Fearing the house would be submerged, at least the lower floor by the rising waters, they began to wake the children.

"We called up all the others and told them to put on their old and warmest clothing." Hurrying out of the house they found it was ". . . entirely surrounded with seething angry waves. This was before 6 a.m. in the dim gray of morning, all the Island wrapped in sleep."

Gilchrist led the way holding on to his youngest daughter Annie and her friend Phoebey Gadsen. She was blown away from him some thirty feet by the winds, ". . . like a leaf and thrown on her face in the water. I rushed after her and got her up. The others were behind me struggling against the wind.

"To recover breath and get strength for a new start we gathered together in a small room in an outbuilding next door to us, but when we all got there we thought it safest to remain until the storm abated and the tide went down." They waited together for an hour when a friend of Emma's showed up to offer help.

". . . dressed in a bathing suit with his head bound with a towel . . . He was heaven sent, for not long after the surging water boiled around the house and penetrated the floor." Gilchrist believed their lives were in danger if they stayed so Emma's friend offered to take the children.

"First he took Phoebey, and by great effort fought his way to the second house to the rear. In fifteen minutes he returned exhausted. When he recovered a second time he started then with Annie. I hung out of the window and watched them until they were lost to sight in the thick and blinding mist."

Elsewhere on the island others were waking up to the storm, the wind drowning the children's cries, as family members clung to each other, trying to decide what to do. Emma's friend had returned and he and Gilchrist were also discussing what to do next when "the report of something like a pistol shot followed by the screams of women started me to the door.

"On looking out I saw the whole Ilwey family, who like ourselves had taken refuge in this kitchen. Struggling up to their armpits in the water, men, women and children, and on looking up I saw the building going to pieces. In a moment we too were in the water battling with the waves and a terrific wind."

"Burdell took care of Emma. Little Gussie took Pippo in her arms, I took Gussie and she held Robbie. Addie struggled by my side. Every yard seemed a mile, the howling wind drowned every voice. As we were thus struggling on Gussie stepped in a hole and fell on her face. Robbie clinging terror stricken to her."

"Hardly had I helped her to her feet when I heard Addie calling 'I am drowning' and on looking round I saw her also down. I pushed Gussie and Robbie to a fence near at hand and told them to cling to it for support while I went to help Addie. I got her on her feet and carried her to the fence. We clung to it as far as it went and then breasted the waves across another street."

Young Burdell had found a safe house to leave Emma and her sisters and returned to take charge of Addie. "So I had only Gussie and Robbie to look after. In not many minutes longer tho they seemed hours we were housed. There we found men, women, children and babies, some of the women were fainting and sick—the babies were crying. The children terrified."

Someone brought out a bottle of whiskey ". . . and all thankfully partook." Burdell after rescuing so many from the angry waters was "used up and required the attention of several ladies." In a roomful of old and young wet to the skin—some better off in their bathing suits—in a house on Middle Street that Gilchrist felt trembled as if they were in a cradle, they were a frightened gathering. Outside the wind "howled as an angry demon thursting for our blood."

Gilchrist was anxious, thinking they were not much better off than what they had left. Those who had recently joined them were satisfied to have shelter, but he knew the tide should be changing at that hour.

". . . but still the waters rose and threatened to engulph the whole island. Everywhere could be seen flying timbers from piazzas and roofs that had yielded to the storm and the waters were filled with their wreck. Large, massive and valuable mansions as well as the humble seaside cottage went over and melted like salt in the waves."

Some of the men began to talk, enchanging ideas and plans about what to do next. They agreed that if the southeast wind continued an hour longer it would force the ocean into the harbor and back up the waters into a tidal wave. They feared then the whole island would be submerged and all would be lost.

"God willed otherwise. At this time of extreme peril the wind shifted in a moment to the West and drove back the angry waters. Gradually they subsided and at 12 dry land appeared."

He and Gussie had been up for eight hours. He wrote his sister, "It was surprising how soon thereafter hunger took the place of fear, and everything eatable was in demand. I went over to our house for a contribution. It was standing intact, tho' a bathing house had left its station and had battered against the piazza like a huge battering ram."

Wind had forced the window panes out and the rain in, and Gilchrist returned to his summer home to find everything wet, but believed that otherwise they would have been safe if they had stayed. "The waves however would have frightened my family to death for they must have pounded against the sides of the house and beat up to the underside of the floor (and) would have been a life time of agony to them and apprehension to me—for God only knew that the house would stand.

"A new house just next to me melted away like salt. Portions of other houses on the other side were blown away like cardboard. There was not a person on island who did not expect my house to be the first to go and I know that some are disappointed that they were not true prophets. I understand that bets were made that it would be so."

Though the house stood, there was considerable damage. A tin roof on the piazza was off and he lost some twenty slates from the main house. Fences all around were down. But his biggest disappointment was the damage done to trees. "My beautiful magnolia and nearly all the wild oranges are down. The product of thirty years wrecked in an hour."

He wrote his sister that her house had escaped wonderfully for the roof was intact and hadn't leaked. Not even her fences were down. "Only the two trees, one by the street and the other in the middle of the garden are broken, but they will recover.

"This has been a blow to the island from which it will take long to recover. Few who experienced the terrors of Tuesday morning will care to run the risk of the same experience. The change, brief as it was, did Gussie a great deal of good, but I doubt if she will go back again. All who can have returned to the city and the season has virtually ended."

Elsewhere in the country that year, New York State passed legislation protecting its mountain resources. Governor David Hill signed a law that established a 681,000-acre Adirondack Forest Preserve with a three-member Forest Commission. That same year the Adirondack Railway made news when a record run of fifty-seven miles was made in fifty-four minutes. The speeding train brought Dr. Durant's son to his dying father's bedside on October 5, 1885.

A local man wrote in his journal the next day. "Tuesday 6 Oct. T. C. Durant is dead, the great rail-road king of North Creek, the engine is draped in mourning, as is also the depot. A great parade because he had a big pile of money, which is not of the least use to him now, he has gone where he cannot take it with him. Neither could it save his life, though his iron horse came with great speed from the city bringing two of the greatest doctors in the country who did their best no dought. But did he have treasures laid up in heaven?"

After Durant's death there were a number of claims for his earthly treasures, some in connection with the operations of the Credit Mobilier. Durant's admirers and critics saw him as either one of America's outstanding builders or as a robber baron. Harold Hochschild wrote, "Like other pioneer American entrepreneurs who were largely a law unto themselves, Dr. Durant was not troubled by moral considerations in his dealings with the public. His practices were characteristic of the period."

Gilchrist might have agreed with that assesment, considering Durant paid less for Gilchrist's land than the original contract called for. Both businessmen were quiet in manner, but the Southerner was a loving and beloved husband and father, concerned with civic activities and the public good. Nowhere is that description found for Durant who lived apart from his family for long periods while he attended to business. *The Glens Falls Republican* of July 15, 1873 reported, "The family of T.C. Durant will return from Europe soon. They have been absent twelve years, during which time the husband and father has seen his family but once."

A year after the hurricane Charleston was hit with another natural disaster. Just after nine o'clock on the evening of August 31, 1886, the first earthquake shock was felt. Others followed and up and down Meeting Street tops of building walls fell to the ground. The portico of the Hibernian Hall crashed to the ground carrying its massive pillars with it.

Fires broke out and people rushed into the streets, afraid to stay in their homes and camping out in tents set up in parks. Some took refuge on ships in the harbor. The earthquake was felt in far away places, including the vicinity of Lake George, Lake Placid and Blue Mountain Lake in the Adirondacks, but nothing like Charleston. Queen Victoria sent a telegram to President Cleveland expressing her sympathies for the loss of life. The cyclone the year before was estimated to cost the city $1,500,000, but the 1886 earthquake damage rose to between five and six million dollars.

At 12 Bee Street the Gilchrist home was on high ground north of the older parts of the city. On one of the fireplace mantels sat the family clock that had been through so many other disasters. Emma may have been the one who wrote in the family journal, "It was thrown by the shock upon a lounge which fortunately stood beneath the mantel. Though seriously injured and some of the gilt ornaments displaced, the fragments were collected and the clock mended, so it is still able to regulate the daily life of its family."

Gilchrist in his thirties had seen action in wartime and narrowly missed being killed. Now in his fifties, he had survived two natural disasters within two years. Perhaps his continued sense of duty came from being thankful to be alive. Perhaps it came from his religious beliefs. Whatever the reason, he continued to be involved in public affairs, and set down on paper what life was like in Charleston in that decade.

CHAPTER FOURTEEN

End of a Century

"Charleston in many respects is far ahead of what she was in 1860—and there is more money here today doing good to the community in a greater number of hands than then." Gilchrist and Paul Hamilton Hayne exchanged several letters before Hayne's death, and this one dated October 14, 1885, told what it was like in the city. Gilchrist was encouraged by what he saw as progress.

"What tho' the old time planter has not as large a bank account, his money was only spent on his own pleasure, his city residence unkempt and did not evidence the wealth of the owner. Now perhaps his house has passed into the hands of a German grocer: but the well painted mansion and beautiful grounds are pleasing to the eye of the stranger." The business community had large numbers of people of German background at the time who dominated the wholesale and retail grocery trade. In Gilchrist's view the German grocer was helping Charleston's image.

He pointed out other changes, comparing another lawyer, Samuel Lord, whose business had suffered, to the factors who "passed thro' the same experience, and there is no business of that sort done now." These agents who transacted business for others were being cut out of the profits.

He wrote what was happening. "Firms like Wagener & Co. advance groceries and dry foods to the country merchant and take their pay in cotton. Hence they monopolize the business. Steamers of large capacity now come to Charleston and in a few weeks take away the whole cotton crop that used to require scores of small sailing vessels, requiring months instead of weeks to do the same business. Hence all those who thrived on the protracted methods of doing business find their occupation gone and are consequently 'blue.'"

He believed, however, that Charleston would remain ahead of Savannah and Wilmington as a seaport and said, "A new and more energetic stock will take the place of the old settlers and will make Charleston what it ought to be."

Specific changes in the city in 1885 were mentioned. "Street cars connecting the termini of the city have taken the place of the rumbling omnibus, fare 5 cents instead of 10 cents. A public supply of water now gives us bath rooms and water closets, and fountains beautify our grounds. A paid fire department now controls fires that reduced insurance 20 percent below 1860 premiums."

Everyday living had improved and Gilchrist explained why. "Marketing is better, cheaper, and at our very doors. Ice is delivered all thro' the day at ½ a cent per lb. Our streets have greatly improved in roadbed and side walks, and in many other respects living is better and easier and cheaper than before the war."

"I speak of these things because I see them, tho like Lord I have many things to discourage me personally. But there is no use in croaking. The problem that we who 'are to the Manor born' can not solve, others tho' strangers will work out in spite of us. Had our people turned in with a helping hand years ago, instead of standing off and snubbing these new men, they also would reap the benefits and Charleston would have kept her place in line with the other cities."

Perhaps he was remembering Uncle Robert's letter when after the war they had discussed the 'Carolina Dignity' which spurned friend and foe alike.

Robert ended the letter to Hayne saying, "Excuse my rambling sheet, but you asked my opinion and I have given it. I love the old city and wish her well." He sent his regards to Mrs. Hayne and signed it, "believe me ever your friend, R.C. Gilchrist."

At the end of the century South Carolina was a far different state from that in which Gilchrist had been born. In 1890 the racist Benjamin Ryan Tillman became governor, entering politics as the self-appointed spokesman of the up-country, poor white farmers. Tillman pushed for agrarian reform and also attempted to push the white aristocracy from power.

Gilchrist was better off than many in Charleston at the time. Along with his law practice, he still had land to sell in the Adirondacks. A lengthy contract signed between Gilchrist and one John McAveigh allowed McAveigh to pay a yearly rent for eight years, allowing him to cut wood for fuel. McAveigh was to "keep the premises in good order and not cut green timber." Gussie was a witness to the signing when they both appeared in Saratoga in October at the height of autumn's colors.

In the Adirondacks, Gilchrist had seen what a railway could bring by way of commercial development. It may have occurred to him when he journeyed for holidays on Sullivan Island that a rail system along the barrier island could bring tourists and business as the Adirondack Railway had done. Although there is little else found, the 1887 city directory of Charleston listed him as president of the Mt. Pleasant and Seaview City Railroad Company with offices at 151 East Bay.

He was also busy with patriotic affairs when he once again accepted the command of the Washington Light Infantry in 1888 at the age of fifty-nine. The following year New York City celebrated the centennial of President Washington's inauguration and the men of his corps said that it was due to Gilchrist's active efforts that they were present and marched in the parade.

By this time memorials, monuments and statues were in place in city parks and courthouse squares in every small town and large city.

On May 29, 1890, there was the unveiling in Richmond of an equestrian statue of the South's favorite general, Robert E. Lee, and Gilchrist and the Washington Light Infantry attended. Of Gilchrist one wrote, "He was also active in promoting the other public-spirited visits to distant cities during recent years when not in active command."

In his own city of Charleston, Gilchrist laid the cornerstone for a new war monument in Washington Square on February 23, 1891 and unveiled the finished memorial in July. It was his last official act before he retired from the Washington Light Infantry. The corps decided at a meeting in the Armory in November that there should be a testimonial acknowledging Gilchrist's many public services.

A resolution was passed that a handsome jewel of military design be presented to him upon his retirement. Made of gold, it was ". . . artistic in design and workmanship, manufactured in this city by Messrs. Stephen Thomas Jr. and Brother. It is suspended from a double spear-head over which a ribbon is draped, upon which is engraved Major Gilchrist's name."

It was a "pendant from a gold chain, an eagle with outstretched wings holds in his talons a six-pointed cross, displaying a six-pointed star for central shield; this is handsomely engraved, with a diamond for its centre."

The testimonial, recalling his many services to the Washington Light Infantry, was printed and sent to Gussie in 1892. From 12 Bee Street she wrote a thank you letter to Mayor William Courtenay telling him: "Your handy work and taste can be traced in the very handsome setting in which the recognition of my husband's services to the W.L.I. have been placed. I appreciate it very highly, and beg you to accept my thanks for this cherished volume."

In 1890, twenty-five years after the Civil War ended, those who had marched off were fading into old men leaning on their canes. Veterans of the war were beginning to die off. Lee had died twenty years before. Grant died in the Adirondacks the summer of the 1885 Charleston hurricane. Beauregard, who had also promoted railroads after the

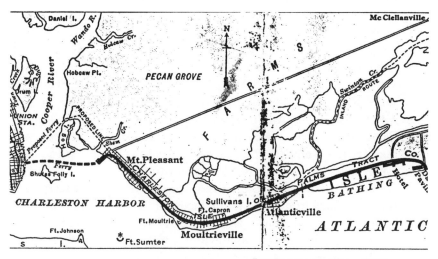

From *Charleston City Directory of 1887*
Proposed line of the Mt. Pleasant and Seaview Railroad Company.

war, died in 1893. Like Gilchrist, they had written memoirs.
The military tradition of the Gilchrist family was being carried on by their only son, Robert Benjamin Gilchrist, as a student at the Citadel. Emma, in her thirties, was sketching and painting and living at home. Annie was at home, too. The second oldest daughter, called Gussie like her mother, married William King McDowell in 1896.

There were other changes. Origin Vandenburg, the New York lawyer who bought Gilchrist's Inglewood mansion and a large amount of his land, had sold off most of the land but not Inglewood. The last twenty years of his life were spent attempting to interest British and American backers in a subway for New York City. After Vandenburg's death in 1892, Inglewood was sold at a sheriff's auction for unpaid taxes and on May 18, 1893, a local lumberman, John Anderson, Jr., purchased lot 46 with the abandoned mansion for $27.61.

Gilchrist was preoccupied with plans for his seashore railway that was to bring ferry passengers from Charleston out to the beaches along the barrier islands. One writer said, "His greatest project, perhaps, was the Seashore Railroad, the forerunner of the present road to the Isle of Palms, which was ruined by the cyclone of 1893." Not only did this second hurricane end his railway plans, it also damaged his island home.

Five years later, in 1898, a new Charleston and Seashore Railroad Company was formed to provide service to Mt. Pleasant, Sullivan's Island, and beyond to the Isle of Palms. Passengers were ferried across the Cooper River to take express trains for the beaches. But it was Dr. Joseph S. Lawrence who was its president and promoter.

"Contracts were entered into for construction of ferry slips in Charleston and Mount Pleasant, a power plant on Sullivan's Island, nearly eight miles of railroad including two bridges, and a dancing pavilion with other recreational facilities at the Long Island (Isle of Palms) end."

Once again Gilchrist was first with an idea that was taken up by someone else. There is no record of his thoughts or feelings about it, and no other information to be found about his 1887 Seashore Railroad. Yet the unfairness of others reaping the fame and fortune that could have been his has the quality of a Greek tragedy. It may be a coincidence that the year Dr. Lawrence's railroad was promoted in 1898, replacing Gilchrist's damaged project, that the Adirondack bridgebuilder suffered a stroke at age sixty-nine.

He had been appointed a city magistrate the year before and after the first severe illness continued with the duties of his office—although he never fully recovered from the stroke.

In deteriorating health, he retired in 1899 to be cared for within the family, no longer leaving the house. The extended family of women devotedly nursed him, as their former caretaker became the cared-for. A sense of putting things in order and settling his affairs meant there was land still to be disposed of in the mountains. On March 7th he conveyed 1,704 acres of remaining Adirondack land to his son for one thousand dollars. Robbie was then twenty-eight, unmarried and living at home.

One of the last Adirondack properties Gilchrist sold was Uncle Robert's home at The Glen. John Anderson Jr. had previously picked up the Inglewood property for taxes. At another sheriff's sale in 1895, Anderson thought he had bought the Gilchrist Glen property. He filed a judgment against Robert for $1,257.36 on June 18, 1895, although it was not recorded until 1899.

If the judgment had been settled, it would account for the fact that The Glen property with its buildings and sixty acres was conveyed from Robert C. Gilchrist to Anderson for only $350 in 1899.

On the eve of a new year and a new century, Robert Cogdell Gilchrist was a stroke vicitm at seventy, confined to his home. Looking back on the old year, Gussie and Robert could recall the wealth of changes they'd lived through in the nineteenth century. How late they stayed up on New Year's Eve, what they talked about, if the children were with them, or who stopped by, is not recorded. There is a record that the family clock was still keeping time in their Charleston home, and would into the new century.

Barely six months in office in 1901, President William McKinley was shot by an angry office seeker. Gilchrist and the recently elected Vice President, Theodore Roosevelt, were distantly related. Both men descended from Claes Martenszen Van Roosevelt, who came to New Amsterdam in 1652 and is generally considered the founder of the family in this country.

From the White House came a small card bordered in black from the White House Secretary thanking Gilchrist for his letter of sympathy to Roosevelt. It is dated September 20, 1901.

Roosevelt had been climbing in the Adirondacks, had been assured that McKinley would recover, but on September 13th he received a telegram that the President was dying. After a wild carriage ride down the steep mountains at night he was told at the North Creek train station that he was now the President. Newspaper stories of the account would remind Gilchrist of his long ago connection to the Adirondack Railway.

His expression of condolences to Roosevelt may have been one of the last things the aging author wrote.

CHAPTER FIFTEEN

The Clock Stops

In the end the Gods were kind in allowing him to die at home in his own bed. He had survived the bullet that parted his hair and momentarily blinded him at Fort Wagner. At the Cheraw bridge blood spurted on him from the man shot at his side. He was still risking his life at war's end at Averysboro and Bentonville, and came near being captured in a hand to hand fight with some of Kilpatrick's cavalry in Fayetteville. And he had lived through the natural disasters that left others dead in Charleston.

Now gathered around his bedside in his last hours would be the grown children beside their mother. He and Gussie had been married for forty of his seventy-three years. The end came at 6:25 on a late Saturday afternoon, August 16, 1902, the doctor listing the cause of death as paralysis. Funeral services were held at home the next day.

In the churchyard cemetery of the Second Presbyterian Church of Charleston there is a Gilchrist plot. The family monuments are enclosed by an iron fence, with the name Gilchrist on the gate. Inside are buried his mother and father, his Uncle Robert of The Glen, Gilchrist's first wife, and two of his infant children by Gussie.

But there is another cemetery. Magnolia Cemetery, the oldest in Charleston not a churchyard cemetery, is on the National Register of historic places. It is where Mary Boykin Chesnut had gone in her carriage at the start of the

Photograph by Wes Pelkey

Monument for parents of
Robert Cogdell Gilchrist.

Photograph by Wes Pelkey

Magnolia Cemetery, Charleston

Photograph by Wes Pelkey

Marble step at entrance to family plot, Magnolia Cemetery.

war and wrote in her diary, "It was hard to shake off the blues after this graveyard business." Burials continue on the grounds today, although not in the glass box she recalled.

It is a beautiful cemetery, with wide avenues that curve around family plots and monuments from another century. Trees are draped in Spanish moss, and bushes and shrubs flower with spring forsythia and azaleas. Magnolias thrive there and the sound of lawnmowers and workmen's clippers indicate the grounds are carefully tended.

This Gilchrist plot is close to the Cooper River. In the ground at the plot entrance is a marble step with the carved letters of the family name. There are several headstones, the tallest an obelisk much weathered and eaten away by air pollution from the oil refineries across the river.

The carved words can barely be made out that say Robert Cogdell Gilchrist, Major in the Confederate States Army. His birthdate and death are listed and then the words that defined his character. "True to every trust. To his God faithful. To his family affectionate. To his country loyal. Sacrificing always interest to conscience. He has entered into 'an inheritance incorruptible and undefiled and that fadeth not away.'"

His sense of decency and duty never left him, old-fashioned and idealistic as it was when all around him men grabbed for wealth arfd power during America's Gilded Age. If in the Adirondacks he was resented for building a bridge the natives believed should benefit them and not an outsider who once fought for the South, his idea showed them the way. It's been written elsewhere, "Strange this need to criticize the ability that is given so few to reach out further than one's fellows. . . ."

Envy may have been behind criticism in both the north and south. He wrote after the 1885 hurricane, "There was not a person on island who did not expect my house to be the first to go and I know that some are disappointed that they were not true prophets. I understand that bets were made that it would be so." Was it because he had been a Unionist and one of the few in Charleston 'of the manor born' financially well off at war's end?

In his letter to the Sunday School teachers he mentions being chastened for tardiness by the accuser's time piece, underlining the word *his* as if it was the only correct time. In the same letter he wrote, "I have endeavored faithfully to discharge my duty to the best of my ability, but I have felt the want of that sympathy and union of purpose. . . ."

He was never described as an ingratiating, hail fellow, well met. In fact, a news account on his retirement from the Washington Light Infantry said, "Of austere and reserved manner, he went his way, doing what he thought right. His record of citizenship is high and might well silence the tongues of the envious."

In Susan Middleton's letter to her cousin Harriet, she repeated gossip about Gilchrist blasting the enemy who shot at him, writing "the gentlemen say this was a shocking waste of powder." Whoever was at the fort to criticize his response when he was fired upon and nearly killed, showed little sympathy for his situation.

Apparently there was also little sympathy for Gilchrist's projects in Charleston after the war, as part of his obituary says, "After the surrender of Johnston's army he returned to Charleston where he has since been identified with the business, political and social life of the city, projecting many schemes which would have greatly advanced the material prosperity of the city had they received sufficient endorsement and encouragement."

Robert Rosen wrote in his *A Short History of Charleston* of the morality play that is Charleston's history. "It resembled the classic Greek tragedy—its aristocratic and noble leaders were plagued by fatal flaws, by hubris, by pride, by something." He could be speaking of Gilchrist.

Yet the Major had his supporters. The Washington Light Infantry men credit him with initiating reconciliation with former enemies. He was honored not only by them, but respected enough to be invited to lay the cornerstone for the war monument at City Hall Park which still stands.

Mayor William Courtenay was his friend whose involve-

ment in Gilchrist's testimonial volume Gussie acknowledged in her thank you letter. Perhaps too, Courtenay was
instrumental in Gilchrist's appointment as city magistrate.

There were other friends. Paul Hamilton Hayne, was a
faithful admirer of Gilchrist, calling him gallant, active,
observant and talented. His *Bivouac* article about Gilchrist's service on Morris Island sings his praises and says
". . . his name deserves to be handed down to posterity as
one of its truest heroes."

Gussie lived on with her unmarried children until
1913. After her death the magnificent home at 12 Bee Street
was sold by her heirs and was large enough to be made into
a maternity hospital. Uncle Robert's home at The Glen, the
last deed in the Adirondacks that his nephew sold, was sold
again in 1900 by Anderson to John McPhillips. He and his
wife, Nora, ran the house as the popular Grove Hotel for
many years. The building burned down in the 1960's.

During the Civil War, Yankee soldiers were billeted in
the home of Gilchrist's sister at Fernandina, Florida. When
the war ended the family returned from Lake City and
eventually regained their house but moved again to North
Carolina when Archibald Baker became president of Floral
College. After his death, Gilchrist's sister lived with her
youngest stepson in Augusta, Georgia. She died in 1904.

In 1911 the state of New York took over the ownership
of the Riverside bridge from the company and the court
awarded them $12,800. A new bridge was erected and is
still in use. The Inglewood mansion in the Adirondacks,
long abandoned after it was sold, passed from John Anderson Jr.'s widow to Elmer Pasco, who took it down so he
could pasture his cows.

Emma, who was old enough to remember summer days
at Inglewood, inherited her father's artistic talent. In a
letter to her brother, Robbie, she wrote, "Some luck came
my way today in three new scholars, so my time is brim full
and if I work hard enough, in a year or so, I shall have the
money for the longed for wheel barrow to carry me sketching in the country." Eventually she had a studio at the

Gibbes Art Gallery which was open to the public when she gave a series of talks on the city and showed her pencil sketches and oils.

Her art exhibit at Jackson, Mississippi, was reviewed by the *Jackson Daily News* saying, "Miss Gilchrist is a member of the Southern States Art League, the Carolina Art Association, the Associated Artists, etc. She was the founder and for many years the president of the Charleston Sketch Club.

"She has exhibited in Washington, Nashville, Savannah, Atlanta, New Orleans, Houston, Jackson, Miami and other cities. Her work has received fourteen first awards and many other honors, including the Lanneau prize for three successive years. She is also a lecturer on the Story of Early Charleston." Emma died in 1929 and was remembered as a small, quiet woman with great energy, much like her father.

In 1926, William King McDowell, husband of the second eldest daughter, Augusta, bought the hospital property at 12 Bee Street and gave it to the Episcopal church as a home for women. McDowell was president of the Coca-Cola Bottling Company in Charleston and also president of the hospital board at the time. He and his wife had no children.

The youngest daughter, Annie, was married to Leger Mitchell, and it was she who donated miniature portraits of the family members to the Gibbes Museum. Her only child died in infancy.

Gilchrist's son, Robert Benjamin Gilchrist, was married late in life to Georgette Holmes. In 1922 their daughter, Mary Gibbes Gilchrist, was born. The city directories of Charleston indicate he was involved in several different businesses. Emma at one point wrote on stationery that listed him as secretary and treasurer of the Mutual Creamery Company.

In 1918 the Charleston directory showed he was vice-president of the Manor Company and cashier and secretary of the Title Guarantee and Deposit Company. A year later he is listed as president of The Liberty Bank and secretary-

Oil painting by Emma Gilchrist of 44 Legare Street, Charleston.

treasurer of Standard Motor Company. By 1923 he was listed as president of the Gilchrist Corporation.

Living at 105 Rutledge Avenue in 1928, the city directory says he was in real estate. Moving from job to job, it appears there with other moves. In a letter to "Dear Robbie" from Emma, she said, "Now that another move is imminent, I feel anxious about the safety of the old silver waiter and coffee urn. You know Mama set such store by them. It would never do to put them in storage where they would surely disappear if not already taken on the transit. Could you suggest to Georgette to give them over to me for safe keeping in my room? and let me know."

Most of the inherited Thurman land that had been conveyed to Robbie before his father died, was sold within a few years. At the height of the Great Depression, Robbie died in April 1930 at age fifty-nine. In 1932 his widow and his two widowed sisters, Augusta and Annie, sold the remaining few pieces of Adirondack land to the Delaware and Hudson Railroad Company.

That year, Mary Gibbes Gilchrist, the only living grandchild of Gussie and Robert, died at age ten. According to her mother the family clock, which had survived so many mishaps, stopped when the little girl died—and could never be made to run again. With her death the line of descendants from Judge Robert Budd Gilchrist and his wife, Mary Gilchrist, ended, and the Gilchrist family clock never again kept time.

The second eldest daughter, Augusta, died in 1936 and was buried next to her husband in the W. K. McDowell plot in front of the Magnolia Cemetery office. Annie, wife of Leger Mitchell, died in 1944 and is buried with her parents and the infant she lost. The son's widow, Georgette, died in 1973 and lies in the family plot at Magnolia. The whereabouts of the clock is unknown.

Gilchrist died before he saw his son's inherited land sold off, perhaps to support a variety of schemes Robbie had become involved in. Like Uncle Robert's disappointment in his only son, the question remains whether Gilchrist

Photograph by Wes Pelkey
Headstone of Mary Gibbes Gilchrist, daughter of Robert B. and
Georgette H. Gilchrist. Last descendant of the Judge and Mary.

would have approved of his own son's business ventures.

In 1947, in a remembrance of his father, Judge Robert Budd Gilchrist, it was written in the Charleston *News and Courier* that he was, "A man of eminent patriotism, inflexible integrity, and an abiding sense of honor and duty. . . ." That could easily describe his public spirited son.

The life and times of Robert C. Gilchrist covered an era of great national growth as well as the passions and sorrows from a fratricidal war. For seventy-three years Gilchrist was inextricably caught up in both.

An Afterword

In the summer of 1987 we moved year-round to Wevertown, New York, where we owned a vacation home. Wide glass and cathedral ceilings keep the house from seeming as small as it is. Sliding glass doors face Gage Mountain and a long and curving drive through stately old maples.

Those long-ago planted trees, and the old boulder and cement foundation our house now sits on, obviously predated our present house. I was curious about that and made an appointment to question Wevertown historian, Lewis Waddell.

He was the first to tell me about the mansion (he and other natives always call it a 'mansion'), built by a Southerner in Wevertown shortly after the Civil War. I could imagine a "Tara" in the Adirondacks at the top of the long drive where our house sits. Then Mr. Waddell added that there had once been a bridge over the Hudson near the property.

My husband and I set out to look for the road that led to the abutments and cables that gave evidence there had once been a nearby bridge. The search for who the mysterious Southerner was and why he came north was on—and my research just beginning.

Mr. Waddell had heard the Southerner's name was Robert Gilchrist and suggested I might find more information by looking through the deeds at the Warren County and Municipal records building. I found there was more than one Robert Gilchrist on the deeds and began to try to sort them out.

In fact I was to discover there were five—and could only keep them straight by middle names and dates on deeds. These listed three of the Gilchrists as coming from Charleston, South Carolina. Census records revealed a Robert C. Gilchrist living in the Town of Johnsburg, New York, (where Wevertown is a hamlet), on July 14, 1870. It gave his age as forty. By far this Robert Gilchrist bought and sold more land according to the deed books, than any other.

Given a date of 1870, I grew more excited about unraveling his story when I went through old newspapers that were on microfilm at the Crandall Library in Glens Falls. *The Glens Falls Republican* of 1871 had two articles about a bridge opening giving Robert C. Gilchrist's name and the name of the engineer who built the bridge. Mr. Waddell also let me see and copy two old letters given to him that mentioned Gilchrist and the bridge's opening.

At New York's State University at Albany library I looked through copies of the *South Carolina Historical Magazine* and found there were Gibbes-Gilchrist family papers located at the South Carolina Historical Society in Charleston.

We made plans to go to Charleston in March 1989. In our Charleston hotel the night before we were to search through the Society's papers, I had trouble sleeping. I was sure I would find a diary or letters that would reveal more about the bridge and what happened to it. I did not.

Instead I read a family journal that documented the genealogy I had pieced together, and read letters that revealed much about the personality of the man who had built the first suspension bridge across the Hudson River. I also discovered he had been many things—artist, attorney, author, antebellum aristocrat, and a Confederate officer. His wife had been a Gibbes and the Gibbes Art Museum was on the same street as the Historical Society.

The assistant Curator of the Gibbes Museum, Angela Mack, met with me and said there was an oil painting of Robert Cogdell Gilchrist, although it was not on display. The only likeness of the Adirondack bridgebuilder comes from that painting. Photographs of other family members are from the museum's miniature portrait collection, although none to be found of Gussie.

Returning home I continued to write to libraries, archives and manuscript departments and individuals who might give me information on Gilchrist. The author of *Old North Country Bridges*, Richard Sanders Allen, not only answered my query, but continued to send suggestions and leads. He eventually came from Albany to see the abutments and cables of this north country bridge he hadn't known existed. It was Mr. Allen and also Mr. Edward Keyes, former ironworks consultant for Hudson-Mohawk Industrial Gateway, who theorized where materials might have come from and what the bridge might have looked like. Mr. Allen also knew the bridge's engineer had graduated from Rensselaer Polytechnic Institute.

At the archives department of R.P.I.'s library I found much about Charles Mac Donald the engineer, but no mention of his building Gilchrist's bridge. I wrote to his Canadian home town of Gananoque where there is a museum holding his papers, but they found nothing regarding this particular bridge. It is for this reason there are so few conclusions about the building of the bridge.

There is not a great deal written about how the competing bridge at Riverside was built either. Again Mr. Allen was helpful in suggesting a piece of New York State legislation about that bridge. After looking in New York State law books I found how the town of Schroon Lake bought stock to insure its completion.

Inevitably I was forced to find out something about bridges—a topic I had never been curious about before— and how they're built. Bridgebuilding has a marvelous history and brought me to the Roeblings and their contributions in spanning the obstacles of an earlier America.

I believe Gilchrist thought his bridge would enable him to secure a depot on the Adirondack Railway from Dr. Durant, and went through the Durant papers searching for some connection to, or mention of, Gilchrist at the Adirondack Museum library at Blue Mountain Lake. What there is regarding Durant's Adirondack Railway makes no mention of the Southerner, although a transfer of land between them is recorded in a deed at the Warren County records room.

The description of the Gilchrist mansion comes from the memories of Grace Harrington Stanley, Hazel Harrington Smith, Pauline Davison Waddell, and Mr. James A. Murphy. Now in their late eighties and nineties, these natives went through the house as children when the mansion stood abandoned. Their most vivid memory is the beautiful view of the Hudson River from the house on the hill. Today trees have grown up to block that view.

At the South Carolina Historical Society I was told Paul Hamilton Hayne had written about Gilchrist. Through inter-library loan I ordered Rayburn S. Moore's *A Man of Letters in the Nineteenth-Century South, Selected Letters of Paul Hamilton Hayne*, and then wrote to Professor Moore at the University of Georgia. I am indebted to him for his help in suggesting that letters between Gilchrist and Hayne might be located at Duke University.

The manuscript department there photocopied three letters by Gilchrist. Written after he returned to the South they revealed much about the man and the changes in post-bellum Charleston. War experiences not mentioned in other places were also found in those letters.

Best of all was Gilchrist's account of the "Defense of Morris Island" included in *The City of Charleston Yearbook 1884*. The fighting that he survived on Morris Island outside of Charleston became the story filmed in the movie, "Glory." While the movie tells the forgotten story of the first Black soldiers to fight for the Union in the attack on the fort at Morris Island, Gilchrist's essay describes what it was like for the defenders.

Mrs. Augusta McDowell Ball wrote to me from Sullivan's Island after I located her through a genealogist, Solomon Breibart. It was Mrs. Ball who was named for the Gilchrist infant listed on the Johnsburg census of 1870. In her letter she said that Julia Augusta Gilchrist married William King McDowell in 1896. She was told that because they had no children, her parents decided to honor "Aunt Gussie" by naming her Augusta. It was in this way that I discovered there were no other direct descendants of Gussie and Robert Cogdell Gilchrist, and I could complete the family tree.

My letter sent to the historical society at Fernandina, Florida was passed on to a descendant of the Reverend Archibald Baker, the widower who married Gilchrist's sister. Mrs. Celeste Kavanaugh, his great-granddaughter, answered my letter with family history indicating Gilchrist's sister was equally brilliant. That she had no children of her own meant Mary and Robert Budd Gilchrist's line ended with the death of the ten-year-old Mary Gibbes Gilchrist in 1932.

The story of the family clock comes from an interview in 1968 with the son's widow by Mrs. A. Waldo Jones of Atlanta, Georgia, and was given to the South Carolina Historical Society. Other tales of the clock are found in the family journal. I tried unsuccessfully to locate Mrs. Jones, and could only wonder if she was distantly related.

On a second trip to Charleston we were invited into the home at 4 John Street by its present owner, Bob E. James, who just happened to be walking by as we were taking pictures of the Gibbes home where Gussie and Robert held their wedding reception. His gracious Southern hospitality enabled me to describe the rooms of that beautiful house which some believe was designed by Manigault.

On only one occasion did I sense resentment toward me as a Yankee. To experience that some 125 years after Gilchrist came to the Adirondacks brought home his courage in coming north so soon after war's end, and what he faced by initiating reconciliation between former enemies.

At first I was simply curious as to what kind of a Southerner would come to the North so soon after the war to build a large home here. Where could the money have come from? Why would he come and what would he face? What was life like then? Over time I grew to believe what I had uncovered was a life story of great courage that deserved to be told.

Endnotes

CHAPTER ONE

Page 1   Adam Gilchrist and his wife Mary Butcher: Family history found in journal in Gibbes-Gilchrist papers at South Carolina Historical Society, Charleston.

Page 2   Robert Budd Gilchrist . . . passed the bar in 1818.: Wilson, *Appleton's Cyclopedia of American Biography*, p. 647.

Page 7   The clock was supported by marble pillars: Jones interview donated to the South Carolina Historical Society and with the Gibbes-Gilchrist papers.

Page 7   "Square after square was demolished": Josiah Bailey, April 18, 1838, "Destructive & Awful Conflagration & Loss of lives," South Carolina Historical Society.

Page 8   "Woman For Sale,": *The Charleston Courier*, Sept. 19, 1843.

CHAPTER TWO

Page 11   ". . . the traditional geography lesson:" Writers Program, *South Carolina, A Guide To The Palmetto State*, p. 185.

Page 11   Billy Green came to the. . .: Family journal, Gibbes-Gilchrist family papers, South Carolina Historical Society, Charleston.

Page 13   "If by making the art your profession:" Rutledge, *Artists in the Life of Charleston*, p. 136.

Page 13   "His art instincts were strong:" Hayne, *The Southern Bivouac*, March 1886, p. 599.

Page 15   This double portrait of Gilchrist as a child with his sister is in the collection at the Gibbes Museum, Charleston, S.C.

Page 16   "Admission to the College of Charleston": From "A Catalogue of the Trustees, Faculty and Students of the College of Charleston, South Carolina, April 1847" located at the Robert Scott Small Library archives, College of Charleston.

Page 17   Judge Gilchrist's letter to his daughter found with the Gibbes-Gilchrist papers.

Page 18   Petigru had recently moved to a new office building designed to resemble a Greek temple: Carson, *Life, Letters & Speeches of James Louis Petigru*, p. 67.

Page 18   He initiated the idea for a YMCA: Obituary, *News & Courier*, August 17, 1902.

Page 18   Letter from Robert Budd Gilchrist to his son August 29, 1854, Gibbes-Gilchrist papers.

Page 19   Gilchrist's first wife, Julia Whitridge, died in 1855. Little is known about her other than that she is buried in the Gilchrist plot of the churchyard of the Second Presbyterian Church, Charleston.

Page 19   The printed letter to the Sunday School Teachers of the Second Presbyterian Church, December 1859, is in the manuscript collection, folder 285, at the South Carolina Historical Society, Charleston.

Page 20   Gilchrist served as a witness to a legal paper: Deed Book 16, pp. 519-523, Warren County, N.Y. records.

CHAPTER THREE

Page 21   "I would not part from my sisters . . .": Carson, *Life, Letters & Speeches of James Louis Petigru*, p. 127.

Page 21   They were one of 28 Charleston companies of part time soldiers: Arthur Wilcox, *The Civil War at Charleston*, p. 3.

Page 24   "A great proportion of our sick soldiers are boys": *News & Courier*, October 15, 1861, p. 1.

Page 24   "If the weather permits, will Miss Augusta take a ride with me. . . .": Gibbes-Gilchrist papers.

Page 24   "We drove to Magnolia Cemetery . . .": Chesnut, p. 29.

Page 25   "A Lady's Experience Inside the Forts in Charleston Harbor During the War": Manuscript Collection, South Carolina Historical Society, Charleston.

Page 25   "My Dear Sue": Gibbes-Gilchrist papers.

Page 26   The Gibbes family genealogy is found in the *South Carolina Historical & Genealogical Magazine*, April 1911, pp. 77-105.

Page 26   "Thank God for pine knots": Chesnut, p. 153.

Page 28   "Charleston is in flames . . .": Ibid, p. 173.

Page 28   Gilchrist raised the Gist Guards artillery: Gibbes-Gilchrist papers.

Page 29   The fighting at times was hand to hand . . .: Warren Ripley, *The Civil War at Charleston*, p. 34.

CHAPTER FOUR

Page 31   "If the enemy will be so kind as to wait": Chesnut, *A Diary From Dixie*, p. 259.

Page 31   Letter from R. C. Gilchrist to wife: Gibbes-Gilchrist papers.

Page 32   "Skirting along ship channel . . .": Robert C. Gilchrist, "Confederate Defense of Morris Island," *City of Charleston Yearbook 1884*, p. 350.

Page 32   Quotations are from his essay.

Page 32   Other sources regarding the defense of Morris Island are: Warren Ripley, *The Civil War at Charleston*, pp. 51-61; John Harleston, "Battery Wagner on Morris Island 1863," *South Carolina Historical Magazine*, January 1956, pp. 1-13; and John Johnson, *The Defense of Charleston Harbor*, pp. 86-153.

Page 35   Susan Middleton's July 13th letter to her cousin: "Middleton Correspondence 1861-1865," *South Carolina Historical Magazine*, July 1963, p. 162.

Page 37   . . . leaving the family clock with a German family named Wittpen: Gibbes-Gilchrist papers.

CHAPTER FIVE

Page 41   Mrs. Chesnut paid $24 for six spools of thread: Chesnut, *A Diary From Dixie*, p. 389.

Page 41   It took five Union Army regiments: *New York Times*, January 7, 1990, p. 20.

Page 42   Gilchrist was detached from his command to serve as Judge Advocte General: Gibbes-Gilchrist papers.

Page 42   "Atlanta is gone": Chesnut, p. 434.

Page 42   Confederate forces had evacuated Charleston: Wilcox, "Charleston is Abandoned," *The Civil War at Charleston*, pp. 76-7.

Page 43   Gilchrist burned the bridge at Cheraw: Robert C. Gilchrist letter to Paul Hamilton Hayne, October 31, 1885, Manuscript Department, Wm. R. Perkins Library, Duke University.

Page 43   As such he signed with the Yankee officer the paroles of the remaining Confederate army: Ibid.

Page 43   Gilchrist's northern uncle . . . conveyed 1,345 acres to an Albany firm: Warren County records, Deed Book 12, p. 68.

Page 45   . . . his securities were in such railroad bonds as Illinois Central: The personal estate and household inventory of Robert Gilchrist of The Glen found in Will #776 at the Warren County Probate Court.

Page 47   "I have entirely recovered from the effects of my last attack of chills and fever": Gibbes-Gilchrist papers.

Page 47   ". . . as to the moiety hereby bequeathed. . .": Will of Mary Gilchrist, Book B, pp. 741-742, Reference room, Charleston County Library.

CHAPTER SIX

Page 49   Gilchrist's maternal grandmother, Elizabeth Roosevelt Gilchrist, had inherited land from the divided estate of her uncle
John Thurman. Deed Book G, p. 83, Warren County records.

Page 49   ". . . times were dull and trade light": Wm. H. Hill, editor,
The Gibson Papers: History of Washington County, New York,
p. 57.

Page 49   What history of Thurman can be found comes from the above
and H.P. Smith, editor, *A History of Warren County 1885*, and
Wm. H. Brown, editor, *A History of Warren County, 1963*.

Page 52   "We have only a few scraps of paper to tell us anything about
this wonderful man": Roger G. Kennedy, *Orders from France*,
pp. 54-57.

Page 52   John Thurman letter to William Cameron: Letter Book at the
New York State Library, Albany.

Page 54   . . . it wasn't until August 25, 1843, that the large Thurman
holdings were finally settled: Letters of Administration #271,
Warren County Probate Court.

Page 55   Described as "of almost unbounded business capacity": Robert
Gilchrist obituary found in the Gibbes-Gilchrist papers.

Page 56   "My Dear Gussie,": Gibbes-Gilchrist papers.

Page 56   By 1863 Dr. Durant and some New York City investors looked
to build a line between Saratoga and North Creek: Smith, pp.
292-3.

Page 56   Other history of Durant's Adirondack Railway can be found in
Harold K. Hochschild's *Doctor Durant and His Iron Horse*, an
Adirondack Museum extract from his privately printed *Town-
ship 34*.

CHAPTER SEVEN

Page 59   . . . New York State bought 700 acres of forest in Clinton County to supply wood for the prison system: Janis Barth, "Wilderness For Sale," *Syracuse Herald American*, December 18,
1988, p. C5.

Page 60   The year 1816 was called the Year Without Summer: H.B.
Smith, ed., *A History of Warren County*, p. 196. Also *The
Essex County Republican*, June 25, 1891.

Page 60   ". . . my two cows filled six tin pans": Robert Gilchrist to Robt.
Cogdell Gilchrist, June 17, 1867, Gibbes-Gilchrist papers.

Page 60   Images of forested mountains . . .: Descriptions and history of
the Adirondacks are found in many sources. Two of the best
are *Adirondack Country*, by Wm. Chapman White, and *The
Adirondack Reader*, Paul Jamieson, editor.

Page 62   "Immediately at hand is a boundless supply of the finest of hardwood . . .": *Glens Falls Republican*, September 19, 1871.

Page 63   By 1840 there were 270 tanneries in the Adirondacks: Jane Eblen Keller, *Adirondack Wilderness*, p. 83.

Page 63   ". . . a Central Park for the World": Jamieson, p. 85.

Page 64   It represents 20 percent of New York State: Barth, p. C5.

Page 65   . . . and called it Inglewood: Gibbes-Gilchrist papers.

CHAPTER EIGHT

Page 67   "Persons wishing to take passage . . .": *The Courier*, Charleston, September 16, 1843.

Page 67   This line was the first . . .: "Railways in the United States," *Encyclopedia Britannica*, Vol. 18, p. 1106.

Page 69   When the entire line was completed: Ibid.

Page 69   . . . the company was kept from laying tracks to the wharves by the city fathers: George C. Rogers, *Charleston in the Age of the Pinckneys*, p. 160.

Page 72   "Last Tuesday the wind gathered all the spare snow . . .": *The Glens Falls Republican*, March 26, 1872.

Page 72   "A train on the Adirondack Railroad recently converted a yoke of oxen . . .": *The Glens Falls Republican*, October 17, 1871.

Page 73   . . . in 1851 there were 8,836 miles of road operated by railroads: *Historical Statistics of the United States*, p. 723.

Page 74   The company had spent six million getting the line into operation: Harold K. Hochschild, *Doctor Durant and His Iron Horse*, p. 9.

Page 74   "It is a notorious fact that there is no country . . .": H.J. Hopkins, *A Span of Bridges*, p. 114.

Page 74   ". . . the trade and travel of the whole country around . . .": *The Glens Falls Republican*, Sept. 12, 1871.

Page 76   It was Washington Roebling's second wife . . .: Samuel Gaillard Stoney, *Charleston, Azaleas and Old Bricks*, plate XXVII.

Page 76   MacDonald became a highly respected bridge builder: *Transit 1897*, p. 7, RPI archives.

CHAPTER NINE

Page 79   Speculation on how components were assembled for the bridge comes from Richard S. Allen, author of *Old North Country Bridges*.

Page 82   The will said . . .: Will of Robert Gilchrist, #776 Probate Court, Warren County.

Page 82   Spencer petitioned to have his cousin execute the Deed of . . .:
Miscellaneous records Book 2, p. 208, Warren County records.

Page 83   Robert bought his cousin, Spencer, a house at . . .: Deed Book
21, pp. 196-8, Warren County records.

Page 85   They walked to the grand opening of Gilchrist's bridge some
two miles away: Eda Russell, "Reminiscences of Clarence Ross
75 Years Ago," *North Creek Enterprise*, June 4, 1941.

Page 85   "A Wire Bridge Across the Hudson": *The Glens Falls Republican*, September 19, 1871.

Page 87   Signed with the initials G.L.S . . .: Ibid.

CHAPTER TEN

Page 89   He owned the *Ellen*, a steamship that traveled . . .: Smith,
History of Warren County, p. 602.

Page 89   Three directors of the newly organized Folsom . . .: "Articles
of Association of the Folsom Landing Central Bridge," Adirondack Museum Library, Blue Mt. Lake, N.Y.

Page 89   An Adirondack Railway brochure related . . .: Frank H.
Taylor, *Birch Bark From the Adirondacks: From City to Trail*,
p. 16.

Page 90   Locke and his son Lorenzo owned the Pottersville Hotel:
Smith, p. 547.

Page 90   . . . it was Aldrich who introduced legislation . . .: Smith, p.
418. Also Brown, *A History of Warren County*, p. 200.

Page 90   ". . . to legalize the acts of the taxpayers . . .": *Laws of NYS
Passed at the 94th Session of the Legislature 1871*, p. 1933.

Page 91   The company charged three cents to walk . . .: Brown, p. 69.

Page 93   Origin Vandenburgh was an attorney . . .: *New York Times*,
Obituary, September 12, 1892.

Page 96   . . . Origin Vandenburgh sold most of the land . . .: Deed
Book 26, p. 128, Warren County records.

Page 98   The excellence of the passenger service . . .: Taylor, pp. 13-16.

CHAPTER ELEVEN

Page 99   "I think I stated in a former . . .": Robert Gilchrist to Robert
Cogdell Gilchrist, June 17, 1867, Gibbes-Gilchrist papers.

Page 101   "The trouble is with the people not the place": Robert C.
Gilchrist letter to Paul Hamilton Hayne, October 14, 1885,
Wm. R. Perkins Library, Manuscript Department, Duke
University.

Page 101   "Being a Union man he was proscribed politically . . .": *News
and Courier*, Obituary, August 17, 1902.

Page 101   "At the close of the war, when South Carolina was . . .": Ibid.

Page 102   "There are many senior members who will quickly . . .": *A Testimonial of Public Services: The Washington Light Infantry to Major R. C. Gilchrist*, pp. 3-4.

Page 102   "A number of items were sent from Boston to be sold . . .": Newton B. Jones, "The Washington Light Infantry at the Bunker Hill Centennial," *South Carolina Historical Magazine*, Vol. 65, 1964, p. 196.

Page 102   ". . . no such scene has ever been witnessed in Charleston before or since": *News and Courier*, Obituary of Robert C. Gilchrist, August 17, 1902.

Page 103   Chamberlain sent the flag . . .: Jones, p. 197. This article is the source for descriptions and quotations of the Washington Light Infantry and the exchanges between former enemies.

Page 103   . . . they were in fact the pet company . . .: Jones.

Page 105   Public eloquence on a momentous occasion in . . .: Speech by R. C. Gilchrist to the Comrades of Massachusetts and New York. Gibbes-Gilchrist papers.

CHAPTER TWELVE

Page 107   ". . . and once inside could see the Roebling display with its sample section of cable . . .": David McCulloch, *The Great Bridge*, p. 350.

Page 108   "The idea of a Centennial . . .": Newton B. Jones, "The Washington Light Infantry at the Bunker Hill Centennial," *South Carolina Historical Magazine*, Vol. 65, 1964, p. 203.

Page 108   "It was during his command of the Rifle Club . . .": *A Testimonial of Public Services: The Washington Light Infantry to Major R. C. Gilchrist*, Charleston, 1892, pp. 3-4.

Page 109   "Some years after he left the White House . . .": Jones, p. 195.

Page 111   The three-story Greek Revival . . .: Robert P. Stockton, "12 Bee St. Is To Be Sold," *News and Courier*, January 27, 1975.

Page 111   "The want of an armory and headquarters . . .": *News and Courier*, Obituary, August 17, 1907.

Page 112   "Had some shrewd Gitana ventured to foretell . . .": Paul Hamilton Hayne, "The Defense of Fort Wagner," *The Southern Bivouac*, p. 599.

Page 114   ". . . on approaching the ditch they broke . . .": Robert C. Gilchrist, "The Defense of Morris Island," *The City of Charleston Yearbook of 1884*, p. 368.

Page 114   "I thank you for your flattering notice of me . . .": Robert C. Gilchrist to Paul Hamilton Hayne, March 1, 1886, Wm. R. Perkins Library, Manuscript Department, Duke University.

CHAPTER THIRTEEN

Page 115   But on August 24, 1885, the official weather forecast for the
. . .: R.L. Schreadley, "The Hurricane of 1885", *News and
Courier*, August 1, 1982.

Page 115   In a letter to his sister . . .: R.C. Gilchrist to Mary Elizbeth
Baker, August 28, 1885, Gibbes-Gilchrist papers. Quotes
describing their experience of the storm come from this letter
throughout the chapter.

Page 116   Back in the city a violent thunderstorm . . .: Schreadley.

Page 120   Governor Hill signed a law that established a 681,000-acre
Adirondack . . .: Janis Barth, "Wilderness For Sale," p. C5.

Page 120   "Tuesday, 6 Oct. T.C. Durant is dead . . .": Diary of David
Dodge, courtesy of Lewis Waddell, Wevertown historian.

Page 120   "Like other pioneer American entrepreneurs . . .": Harold K.
Hochschild, *Doctor Durant and His Iron Horse*, p. 14.

Page 121   Just before nine o'clock . . .: "A Descriptive Narrative of the
Earthquake of August 31, 1886," *City of Charleston Yearbook 1886*, Charleston.

CHAPTER FOURTEEN

Page 123   "Charleston in many respects is far ahead . . .": Robert C.
Gilchrist letter to Paul Hamilton Hayne, Wm. R. Perkins
Library, Manuscript Department, Duke University.

Page 123   The business community had large numbers of people of German background . . .: Robert Rosen, *A Short History of
Charleston*, p. 128.

Page 125   McAveigh was to "keep the premises in good . . .": Deed
Book 43; pp. 439-443, Warren County records.

Page 125   . . . and the men of the corps said . . .: *A Testimonial of
Public Services: The Washington Light Infantry to Major
R.C. Gilchrist*, p. 4.

Page 126   . . . Gilchrist laid the cornerstone . . .: *News and Courier*,
Obituary, August 17, 1902.

Page 126   From Bee Street she wrote a thank you letter to Mayor Wm.
Courtenay . . .: Mary Augusta Gilchrist to Mayor Courtenay,
March 19, 1902, The South Caroliniana Library, Manuscript
Division, University of South Carolina, Columbia.

Page 127   . . . on May 18, 1893, a local lumberman, John Anderson, Jr.,
purchased . . .: Deed Book 68, pp. 524-5, Warren County
records.

Page 128   "His greatest project, perhaps, was the Seashore Railroad, the
forerunner of the present road to the Isle of Palms . . .: *News
and Courier*, Obituary, August 17, 1902.

Page 128   Contracts were entered into for construction of ferry slips . . .:
W.W. Wanamaker, *Long Island South*, p. 223. Also Jane E.
Allen, "Do You Know Your Charleston?", *Post-Courier*,
January 10, 1983, p. 1-B.

Page 128   On March 7th he conveyed 1,704 acres . . .: Deed Book 87,
pp. 172-3, Warren County records.

Page 129   Gilchrist and the recently elected Vice-President . . .: FDR
Library, National Archives and Records Service, Hyde Park,
NY

CHAPTER FIFTEEN

Page 131   The end came at 6:25 on a late Saturday . . .: "Major R.C.
Gilchrist, Death of a Gallant Soldier and Eminent Citizen,"
News and Courier, August 17, 1902.

Page 131   . . . the cause of death paralysis: Death records, Reference
Department, Charleston County Library.

Page 133   "It was hard to shake off . . .": Mary Boykin Chesnut, *Diary
From Dixie*, p. 29.

Page 133   "Strange this need to criticize the ability . . .": Mary S.
Lovell, *The Sound of Wings*, p. 191.

Page 134   "Of austere and reserved manner . . .": News clipping with
W.L.I. Testimonial without source or date. According to
Herbert J. Hartsook, Curator of Manuscripts at the South
Caroliniana Library, University of S.C., Columbia, "This is
common for such items."

Page 134   Susan Middleton's letter to her cousin, Harriet . . .: "Middleton Correspondence 1861-1865," *South Carolina Historical
Magazine*, Vol. 64, July 1963, p. 162.

Page 134   Robert Rosen wrote in his *A Short History of Charleston*, p. 6.

Page 135   Paul Hamilton Hayne, *The Southern Bivouac*, p. 599.

Page 135   After her death the magnificent home . . .: Robert P.
Stockton, "12 Bee Street is To Be Sold," *News and Courier*,
January 27, 1975.

Page 135   Uncle Robert's home at The Glen . . .: Deed Book 87, pp.
389-90, Warren County records.

Page 135   Gilchrist's sister Mary Elizabeth Baker died in 1904. Letter
from Celeste Kavanaugh to the author, October 27, 1990.

Page 135   "Some luck came my way . . .": Gibbes-Gilchrist papers.

Page 136   "She has exhibited in Washington . . .": Miscellaneous news
clippings on Emma Gilchrist, Gibbes-Gilchrist papers.

Page 136   In 1926 William King McDowell . . .: Stockton.

Page 139   "Dear Robbie,": Gibbes-Gilchrist papers.

Page 139   In 1932 his widow and his two widowed sisters . . .: Deed Book
            189, p. 401, Warren County records.

Page 139   According to her mother the family clock . . .: Interview with
            Georgette Gilchrist, on November 1968 by Mrs. A. Waldo
            Jones, given to the South Carolina Historical Society,
            Charleston.

Page 139   The second eldest daughter, Augusta, died . . .: Letter from
            Augusta MacDowell Ball to the author, July 18, 1989.

Page 140   In a remembrance of his father Judge Robert Budd Gilchrist
            . . .: "S.C. Birthdate," *News and Courier*, September 28,
            1947, p. 4.

Bibliography

Allen, Richard Sanders, *Old North Country Bridges*, Utica, New York, North Country Books, 1983.

Articles of Association of Central Bridge Company, Adirondack Museum at Blue Mt. Lake, NY

Brown, William H., (ed.), *A History of Warren County*, Glens Falls, NY: Board of Supervisors, 1968.

Carson, James Petigru, (ed.), *Life, Letters & Speeches of James Louis Petigru*, Washington, D.C.: W.H. Lowdermilk and Co., 1920.

Chase, Harold, et al., *Biographical Dictionary of the Federal Judiciary*, Detroit: Gale Research Co., 1976.

Chesnut, Mary Boykin, *A Diary From Dixie*, Williams, Ben Ames, ed., Boston: Houghton Mifflin Co., 1949.

Drewry, Charles S., *A Memoir of Suspension Bridges*, London: A. & R. Spottiswoode, 1832.

Gibbes-Gilchrist papers, The South Carolina Historical Society, Charleston, SC

Gilborn, Craig, *Durant*, Blue Mt. Lake: Adirondack Museum, 1981.

Gilchrist, Robert Cogdell, "Confederate Defense of Morris Island," *Yearbook of City of Charleston 1884*, Charleston: City of Charleston, 1884.

_____, *The Duties of A Judge Advocate In A Trial Before A General Court-Martial*, Columbia, SC: Evans and Cogswell, 1864.

Hammond, Samuel H., *Wild Northern Scenes*, Harrison, New York: reprinted by Harbor Hill Books, 1979.

Hayne, Paul Hamilton, (ed.), *The Southern Bivouac*, Vol. I, No. 10, March 1886.

Hill, William H., (ed.), *History of Washington County, N.Y.*, The Gibson Papers, Fort Edward, NY: Honeywood Press, 1932.

Historical Statistics of the United States, Washington: U.S. Dept. of Commerce, 1975.

Hochschild, Harold K., *Doctor Durant and His Iron Horse*, Blue Mt. Lake, NY: Adirondack Museum, 1961.

Hopkins, H.J., *A Span of Bridges*, New York: Preager Publishers, 1970.

Jamieson, Paul, (ed.), *The Adirondack Reader*, Glens Falls: the Adirondack Mountain Club, Inc., 1982.

Johnson, John, *The Defense of Charleston Harbor*, Freeport, New York: Books for Libraries Press, 1970.

Jones, Newton B., "The Washington Light Infantry at the Bunker Hill Centennial," *The South Carolina Historical Magazine*, Vol. 65, The South Carolina Historical Society, 1964.

Keller, Jane Eblen, *Adirondack Wilderness: A Story of Man and Nature*, Syracuse: Syracuse University Press, 1980.

Kennedy, Roger, *Orders From France*, New York: Alfred Knopf, Inc., 1989.

Laws of NYS Passed at the 94th Session of the Legislature 1871, Albany: Argus Printers, 1871.

Lovell, Mary S., *The Sound of Wings*, New York: St. Martins Press, 1989.

McCullough, David, *The Great Bridge*, New York: Simon & Schuster, 1972.

Mirkin, Stanford, M., *What Happened When*, New York: Ives Washburn, 1968.

Moore, Rayburn S., (ed.), *A Man of Letters in the Nineteenth-Century*: Selected Letters of Paul Hamilton Hayne, Baton Rouge: Louisiana State University Press, 1982.

Rogers, George C., *Charleston in the Age of the Pinckneys*, Norman, Oklahoma: University of Oklahoma Press, 1969.

Rosen, Robert, *A Short History of Charleston*, San Francisco: Lexikos, 1982.

Rutledge, Anna Wells, *Artists in the Life of Charleston*, Philadelphia: The American Philosophical Society, 1949.

Shaughnessy, Jim, *Delaware and Hudson*, Berkley, California: Howell-North Books, 1967.

Smith, H. B., (ed.), *A History of Warren County*, Syracuse 1885.

Stoney, Samuel Gaillard, *Charleston, Azaleas and Old Bricks*, Boston: Houghton Mifflin, 1939.

A Testimonial of Public Services, The Washington Light Infantry to Major R. C. Gilchrist, Charleston: Walker, Evans & Cogswell, 1892.

Wanamaker, W. W., *Long Island South*, Columbia: South Carolina Printing Co., 1975.

White, William Chapman, *Adirondack Country*, Syracuse University Press, 1985.

Whitney, Charles S., *Bridges: Their Art, Science and Evolution*, New York: Crown Publishers, Inc., 1983.

Wilcox, Arthur M. and Warren Ripley, *The Civil War at Charleston*, Charleston: *The News & Courier*, and *The Evening Post*, 1988.

Wilson, James Wilson and John Fiske, (ed.), *Appleton's Cyclopedia of American Biography*, Vol. II, New York: D. Appleton & Co., 1888.

Writers Program of the Work Projects Administration, *South Carolina, a Guide to the Palmetto State*, New York: Oxford University Press, 1941.

NEWSPAPERS AND PERIODICALS

Charleston Courier, Sept. 16, 1843; Sept. 19, 1843.

Charleston Daily Courier, Oct. 17, 1861.

The Essex County Republican, June 25, 1891.

News and Courier, Aug. 17, 1902; Sept. 28, 1947; Aug. 1, 1982.

Glens Falls Post Star, Nov. 23, 1966.

Glens Falls Republican, Sept. 12, 1871; Sept. 19, 1871, Mar. 27, 1872; Aug. 20, 1872; Apr. 8, 1873.

The New York Times, Sept. 12, 1892; Jan. 7, 1990.

The North Creek News Enterprise, June 4, 1941.

The South Carolina Historical Magazine, Apr. 1911; Jan. 1956; July 1963; Vol. 65, 1964.

Syracuse Herald American, December 18, 1988.

Index

Gilchrist, Robert Augusta, 2, 49
Gilchrist, Robert Benjamin, 84,
    129, 136, 139
Gilchrist, Robert Budd, 2, 4, 7,
    18, 49, 101, 140
Gilchrist, Uncle, 20, 43, 54, 55
Gilmore, General Quincy, 34, 37,
    38
Gist Guards, 28, 32
Glen, The, 45, 46, 54, 59, 97,
    129, 135
Glen Bridge, 55
Glens Falls Republican, 69, 74,
    85, 87, 90, 100, 121, 142
Grant, Ulysses, 41, 81, 107, 126
Great Machinery Hall, 107
Hampton, Anne, 31
Hampton, Wade, 109-111
Hayne, Paul Hamilton, 16, 21,
    26, 112-114, 123, 135
Hudson River, 54, 65, 74, 79, 84,
    97, 142
Hurricanes,
    1885, 115-133
    1893, 128
Inglewood, 65, 74, 81, 96, 127,
    135, 144
Jackson, Andrew, 9, 67, 101
James Island, 28, 32, 39
Johnsburg, 52, 55, 74, 90, 92, 142
Kansas Nebraska Act, 18
Lamboll, Elizabeth, 1
Lincoln, 41, 42, 44, 81
MacDonald, Charles, 76, 85
Magnolia Cemetery, 24, 131, 134
Massachussetts 54th, 113, 144
Mazyckboro, 7
McClellan, George, 41, 96
McDowell, Wm. King, 127,
    136, 139
Meeting Street, 8, 11, 121
Miniature portraits, 4, 5, 14, 46
Morris Island, 29, 32, 43, 111,
    112
Mt. Pleasant & Seaview City
    Railway Co., 125, 127, 128
Murray, Rev. William, 61
National Rifle Association, 102
North Creek, 56, 72, 73, 129
Panic of 1873, 71
Paul Smith, 62

Petigru, James Louis, 8, 18, 21
Philadelphia Centennial, 106, 108
Pope, Thomas, 74
Railroads, 9, 38, 56, 61, 69, 71,
    76, 77, 93, 120
Reconstruction, 44, 99, 109, 114
Riots, 8, 41, 108, 109
Ripley, General Roswell, 25, 32
Riverside, 72, 73, 91, 93, 96-98,
    135
Roebling, Washington, 74, 76
Roosevelt, Nicholas, 49
Roosevelt, Elizabeth, 49
Roosevelt, Theodore, 67, 129-130
Saratoga, 45, 55, 56, 69, 72, 73,
    125
Secessionville battle, 28-29
Second Presbyterian Church
    of Charleston, 19, 27, 132
Sheriff's sales, 127, 129
Slaves, 8, 11, 21, 84, 114
Smyth, Dr., 26
Sons of Liberty, 50
South Carolina Institute, 20, 28
Southern Bivouac, 112. 135
Spencer, Ambrose Judge, 54
Sullivan Island, 29, 39, 115,
    125, 128
Sunday school letter, 19, 134
Tariffs, 1829 & 1832, 8, 9
Testimonial to Gilchrist, 126
Thurman, John, 48, 51, 53, 60,
    64, 72, 85
Tillman, Governor, 125
Totten & Crossfield, 51, 52, 65
Trudeau, Edw. Livingston, 62
Uncle Robert, 20, 43, 54, 55,
    60, 99
VanBuren, President, 7
Vandenburgh, Origin, 93, 94, 127
War of 1812, 1, 6
Warren County Railroad, 45, 55
Washburn's Eddy, 72, 74, 81, 89
Washington Light Infantry, 7, 17,
    101, 106-107, 111, 126, 134
Wevertown cemetery, 2, 54
Whitridge, Julia, 19
Wills, 48, 82
Wilson, Senator, 99
Y.M.C.A. in Charleston, 18
Zouave cadets, 21, 23, 25